Inclusive Outdoor Recreation for Persons with Disabilities

PROTOCOLS AND ACTIVITIES

Donald R. Snyder
Anne Rothschadl
Marcy Marchello

Idyll Arbor

Idyll Arbor, Inc

39129 264th Ave SE, Enumclaw, WA 98022 (360) 825-7797

Idyll Arbor, Inc. Editor: Thomas M. Blaschko
© Copyright 2006 by

Massachusetts Department of
Conservation and Recreation
Universal Access Program
Shared Ventures Outdoors Grant Project

Springfield College
Department of Sport Management and Recreation

Idyll Arbor, Inc.

ISBN-13 9781-882883-64-6
ISBN 1-882883-64-0

Contents

Preface

Inclusive Outdoor Recreation for Persons with Disabilities: Protocols and Activities is intended for students, consumers, and practitioners in Therapeutic Recreation, Outdoor Recreation, and Special Education. Instructors who teach undergraduate and graduate courses can use this text to develop programs, services, protocols, and activities to better serve persons with disabilities in their use of the great outdoors.

The chapters are organized to provide the reader with a progression from general to specific and are intended to provide the means to develop, implement, and evaluate the activities with a variety of populations.

The authors wish to thank the following individuals who provided invaluable feedback and input into this text: Maryann Snyder and Donald R. Snyder Jr. for their love and support, Sandra Bourret for her dedication to healthcare and her passion for reading; Dr. William J. Sullivan, Retired Dean of the School of Graduate Studies, Springfield College for his friendship and professionalism; the faculty in the Department of Sport Management and Recreation at Springfield College; and the staff at Shared Ventures Outdoors who developed, tested, implemented, and evaluated the specific protocols and activities with hundreds of clients over a three-year period.

Special thanks and appreciation should be given to the following agencies and individuals:

Massachusetts Department of Conservation and Recreation
- Thomas J. McCarthy, MLA, ASLA, Universal Access Program Director
- Marcy Marchello, BS, Universal Access Program Coordinator
- Cyndy Chamberland, MSW, LCSW, Universal Access Program Grant Coordinator
- Angela M. Cullinan, BEd, CTRS, Universal Access Program Recreation Facilitator

Springfield College: Department of Sport Management and Recreation
- Donald R. Snyder, EdD, CTRS, Professor and Graduate Coordinator
- Anne M. Rothschadl, PhD, Associate Professor
- Robert Accorsi, MEd, Associate Professor
- Cori L. Adelman, Graduate Student in Therapeutic Recreation Management
- Rebecca L. Krest, Undergraduate Student in Therapeutic Recreation Service
- Akiko Sato, Graduate Student in Outdoor Recreation Management
- Suzanne Serianni, Graduate Teaching Fellow in Outdoor Recreation Management
- Debra Golloboff, Graduate Teaching Fellow in Therapeutic Recreation Management
- Kathryn Henderson, Graduate Teaching Fellow in Therapeutic Recreation Management

This text is a means to "Build Bridges not Fences for Persons with Disabilities" to:

1. appreciate and utilize outdoor recreation areas,
2. fulfill their needs and interest,
3. help eliminate problems and barriers in achieving their outdoor recreation goals.

Sincerely,
Dr. Donald R. Snyder, CTRS
Professor and Graduate Coordinator
Department of Sport Management and Recreation
SPRINGFIELD COLLEGE

Acknowledgments

We would like to thank the park staff at Robinson State Park, Wendell State Forest, the DAR State Forest, Wells State Park, Holyoke Heritage State Park, Mt. Tom State Reservation, and the Connecticut River Greenway State Park and the staff at the Greenfield, Springfield, and Holyoke Skating Rinks for their generous sharing of their limited time and resources to insure that the program sites were in excellent condition and for their hands-on assistance.

The Department of Conservation and Recreation's Boston Office staff Cheryl Brooks, Director of Accounting and Norma Forgione, Federal Grants Officer for their aid in processing all that paper to insure a steady funding stream.

We especially thank other contributing authors, Cynthia Chamberland, Angela Cullinan, and Akiko Sato. Rebecca L. Krest, Suzanne Serianni, and Akiko Sato helped with the diagnosis section.

Finally, we would like to thank the late Regional Director, Carroll Holmes, who was instrumental in originally supporting the Shared Ventures Outdoors project at the conceptual stage and Maryann Snyder for her assistance with the final draft of this text.

Photo Credits

Cover photo: Marcy Marchello

Shared Ventures Outdoors collaborators from the Massachusetts Department of Conservation and Recreation and Springfield College. From left to right: Cyndy Chamberland, Akiko Doi, Tom McCarthy, Marcy Marchello, Dr. Anne Rothschadl, Angie Cullinan, Dr. Donald R. Snyder

Cross-country skiing: Marcy Marchello
Ice-skating: Marcy Marchello
Snowmobiling: Marcy Marchello
Camping: Marcy Marchello
Cycling: Marcy Marchello
Fishing: Marcy Marchello
Accessible hiking: Marcy Marchello
Nature walks: Marcy Marchello
Flatwater paddling: Marcy Marchello
Rowing: Marcy Marchello
Nature photography: Will Blaschko

Chapter One

Introduction

Donald R. Snyder
Cyndy Chamberland
Marcy Marchello

The purpose of this resource manual is to enable therapeutic recreation specialists, outdoor recreation specialists, occupational therapists, physical therapists, special educators, physical educators, recreation professionals, coaches, people with disabilities, curriculum specialists, teachers, and any other concerned individuals to meet the needs, interests, and capabilities of their participants in outdoor activities. This text is designed to grow and change as the profession and activities change. It is to be as dynamic as the individuals who participate in the activities. It is not meant to stereotype clients according to their disability or in any way limit the potential of the individual.

The text and the project were a result of collaboration among the Department of Conservation and Recreation (DCR), Universal Access staff, Shared Ventures Outdoors staff, Springfield College faculty, and Springfield College graduate and undergraduate students. Each contributing agency will be briefly described in this chapter.

Shared Ventures Outdoors

This text was completed to disseminate and support the goals of the Shared Ventures Outdoors Project. The Shared Ventures Outdoors (SVO) Project was a three-year demonstration grant project whose main goal was to expand accessible outdoor recreation for persons with disabilities in Massachusetts. The Massachusetts Department of Conservation and Recreation (DCR) obtained a grant from the United States Department of Education Rehabilitative Services Administration. The grant period was from October 1999 to September 2002. Funding included $291,000 federal dollars and matching funds from the Massachusetts Department of Conservation and Recreation for $368,515. The SVO Program was a collaboration between the Massachusetts Department of Conservation and Recreation, Springfield College's Department of Sport Management and Recreation, Greenfield Community College's Outdoor Education Certificate Program, and Stavros Center for Independent Living. Major objectives for SVO included:

1. Expand the awareness and participation of persons with disabilities in outdoor recreation in Massachusetts.
2. Develop new accessible and inclusive consumer-driven outdoor recreation programs.
3. Train volunteers and students in accessible, inclusive outdoor recreation through experiential learning including volunteer opportunities, internships, and graduate associateships.
4. Increase independence, socialization, mobility, and self-efficacy of participants with disabilities through outdoor recreation.
5. Increase participants with disabilities independent use of outdoor recreation.

A statewide survey on outdoor recreation was completed by consumers with disabilities and their families in 2000. Based on respondents' preferences, interests, and concerns, new accessible outdoor recreation programs were developed and field-tested. The new programs, which are included in this curriculum guide, include fishing, photography, snowmobiling, canoeing, hiking, and camping. Other programs included are nature walks, rowing, kayaking, ice-skating, and cross-country skiing, which are established programs within the Massachusetts DCR Universal Access Program.

Department of Conservation and Recreation

The Massachusetts Department of Conservation and Recreation (DCR) — formerly the Department of Environmental Management — manages the state forest and park system. This includes approximately 300,000 acres of land, which is equal to 5% of the state.

DCR is the state's primary natural resource planning agency and helps to maintain three million more acres of public and private forestlands. DCR's properties range from the Berkshire Mountains to the Atlantic Ocean. Well over 100 facilities, including urban heritage parks, rail trails, beaches, and campgrounds are managed by DCR. Over twelve million people per year visit Massachusetts State Forests and Parks to swim, fish, camp, hike, picnic, sightsee, cycle, ski, skate, paddle, and more.

The mission of the Department of Conservation and Recreation is to exercise care and oversight for the natural, cultural, and historic resources of the Commonwealth and to provide quality public recreational opportunities that are environmentally sound, affordable, and accessible to all citizens.

In 1994, DCR established a Universal Access Program to address the needs of people with disabilities with regard to recreation in state parks and forests. Through ongoing site improvements and adaptive recreation programs, park visitors with disabilities and their families and friends have increasing opportunities to enjoy many different types of recreation and environments year round. The recreation activities listed in this manual are examples of the types of programs that take place within Massachusetts State Forests and Parks.

Springfield College's Department of Sport Management and Recreation

Since its founding in 1885, the Springfield College humanics philosophy has guided the education of the whole person in spirit, mind, and body. All individuals are seen as having extraordinary potential regardless of ethnicity, color, creed, or societal status.

Springfield College has been a pioneer leader in Sport, Recreation, Therapeutic Recreation, and Outdoor Recreation Management for over one hundred years. Springfield College offers programs that provide hands-on opportunities, practica, internships, presentations, and other experiences to promote leadership programming, management, and supervisory experience with **all** individuals. We work with the abilities and the strengths of our consumers. We also build bridges to opportunity helping overcome problems and barriers that can affect one's recreation and leisure lifestyle.

Springfield College offers a Therapeutic Recreation Management program at the bachelor's and master's degree levels. The programs are designed to prepare entry-level, supervisory, and administrative personnel for the field of therapeutic recreation management. The program is competency-based in design and follows the guidelines published by the National Recreation and Parks Association (NRPA) and the National Therapeutic Recreation Society (NTRS). The program embraces the current NTRS vision statement and the curriculum educates students who will ensure that individuals with disabilities or limitations are afforded leisure experiences that enhance their physical, social, emotional, intellectual, and spiritual abilities.

The Therapeutic Recreation Management program emphasizes and provides a variety of skills in clinical and nonclinical settings. Such settings include medical, surgical, and psychiatric hospitals; senior centers; child life programs; mental health agencies; sheltered workshops; vocational training centers; correctional facilities; and long-term care facilities serving persons with a variety of biopsychosocial needs. Graduates of Springfield College's Therapeutic Recreation Management program have completed the educational requirements to be certified by the National Council for Therapeutic Recreation Certification (NCTRC) as a Certified Therapeutic Recreation Specialist (CTRS).

Millions of individuals are involved in recreation activities programs at outdoor facilities. The education of professionally trained outdoor recreation leaders and managers is essential to the field. Springfield College has prepared leaders and administrators for positions in private, profit and not-for-profit sectors such as ski areas and resorts or in public areas such as parks and forests. Graduates of the Outdoor Recreation Management program are eligible for certification as Certified Leisure Professionals (CLP). Springfield College has an outdoor recreation facility and areas used for classroom skill and outdoor experiential learning.

Springfield College's Department of Sport Management and Recreation and Massachusetts Department of Conservation and Recreation are partners in producing this curriculum guide designed to improve the quality of life of persons with disabilities. The curriculum guide is seen as a means for persons with disabilities to reach their personal goals in the great outdoors.

Please remember, recreation is your therapy!!

Dr. Donald R. Snyder

Chapter Two

General Modification and Adaptation Guidelines

Donald R. Snyder

The Outdoor Therapeutic Recreation Process

I believe that all recreation is therapeutic. Therapeutic Recreation provides activities, programs, and services that are voluntary and/or prescriptive in nature to meet the needs and interests of individuals with disabilities.

What is a process? A process in business may be the way an organization conducts itself in order to be efficient. In the human service professions a process can be seen as the best means of providing the biopsychosocial needs of the individual. Efficiency and the biopsychosocial needs of the client are important goals for the specialist in providing for a quality of life that meets the wants and specific needs of the client. In the recreation and park profession we can learn from the private sector and the human service sector by blending these desired outcomes to plan programs with and for clients with various ability levels.

The specialist's major goal is the provision of quality interventions and facilitation techniques to help clients grow and to assist them in meeting their needs and reaching their abilities through outdoor activities and experiences. The needs of the clients dictate where the outdoor therapeutic recreation process will be concentrated. The process (adapted from O'Morrow and Reynolds, 1989) can be listed as six major steps:

1. Assessment of Client
2. Planning of the Overall Program
3. Determining the Evaluation Criteria
4. Implementation of the Program
5. Evaluation of the Program
6. Follow-up of Client's Progress

It is important to establish that the outdoor recreation specialist, therapeutic recreation specialist, and the client work as a team throughout the entire outdoor therapeutic recreation process to determine the best possible program and the most conducive modification and adaptation guidelines.

PROTOCOLS

What is a protocol? In business and medicine a protocol is a standardized means to an end. It is a way to provide a service that is efficient and consistent, to provide the most benefit to the client by the provider. A written protocol can also be implemented by other educated or trained individuals to insure the best results possible.

In an outdoor environment, protocols should be written for all activities and they should be dynamic in nature. These protocols should be reviewed at least annually. In this text, a protocol is defined as a systematic organizational plan to implement a desired outdoor therapeutic recreation activity by providing a meaningful, fun, safe, and consistent means to meet the needs and abilities of the participant.

COMPREHENSIVE ASSESSMENT

Comprehensive assessment in outdoor/therapeutic recreation has been documented in studies by therapeutic recreation specialists. We assess to gain information that is useful and helpful to clients. This assessment should determine the client's values, attitudes, interests, behaviors, strengths, and expectations. Through this process, we can identify the nature and extent of the individual's problems (internal) and barriers (external) to participation. O'Morrow and Reynolds (1989) list a variety of different needs that should be the focus for planning outdoor/therapeutic recreation programs and activities:

- increasing confidence
- feeling a sense of belonging
- learning social or leisure skills
- managing stress
- reducing anxiety
- developing a wholesome body image
- improving fitness
- becoming aware of values
- developing a sense of humor
- enhancing self-esteem

- building positive expectations
- establishing a sense of control
- experiencing fun and enjoyment
- increasing functional skills (e.g. ADL skills)

Confidence is the feeling that provides the client with the drive to continue and re-create the experience. Improving on individual biopsychosocial goals is reached through continued recreative experiences.

Jay B. Nash (1953) in his book *Philosophy of Recreation and Leisure* wrote a chapter on this very topic entitled "Man Must Belong." Belonging is a basic human need.

> When man belongs, he is loyal to his group. This is a basic human need. Those who are beyond the inner circle do not count. They are the foreigners, the family in another group, and the "kid" on the other side of the tracks, or the owner or guardian of goods who is not known. Outsiders are "you and yours," as compared with "mine and ours." Group tensions arise because of differences in customs, ways of living, eating, or dressing, plus of course, ways of worshipping, and differences in language and race (p. 99).

One must be part of the group in order to have the feeling of belonging. All individuals — primitive people, the Athenian youth, the American Indian, today's youth, and persons with disabilities — must have a sense of belonging to be successful citizens of the world. Through the development of protocols that contain appropriate modifications and adaptations to encourage success, we also encourage belonging, a major ingredient for happy and healthy individuals. Experiencing outdoor activities in various outdoor settings provides participants with outlets for their creativity.

We know through research that recreation provides social skills and a variety of leisure and recreation skills that promote a leisure lifestyle conducive to an improved quality of life. The freedom and opportunity that outdoor experiences provide also help manage stress and reduce anxiety from work.

Skill development is the basic premise of education, physical education, recreation, and life in general. We all strive for wholesome body image through activities that provide for fitness, improving strength, agility, range of motion, endurance, cardiovascular, and cardiopulmonary development.

Outdoor recreation experiences encourage value identification and clarification by providing challenges and experiences freely chosen by the client. In group situations, we develop a sense of humor with other individuals based on our and their skills, abilities, and shortcomings identified in real experiences and challenges in the outdoors.

Striving for creativity through challenging activities enhances our self-esteem and our beliefs in what we can do, not what we cannot do. We work with abilities, not disabilities. The belief in our ability builds positive expectations for the challenges that outdoor activities provide. We develop and later establish a sense of being and sense of control. Through our outdoor activity experiences, we can choose those activities that provide us with fun and enjoyment, a product of our success.

Along with the leisure and recreative skills, functional skills and Activities of Daily Living (ADLs) are also products of outdoor activities. Eating, dressing, lifting, rolling, toileting, and moving around are just some examples of skills that are modified, adapted, and practiced in an outdoor setting.

The needs discussed along with other individual needs can be determined through formal and informal comprehensive assessment techniques. Asking the client what he or she wishes to gain from the activity and experience is a most helpful strategy. Also, debriefing exercises in small groups and individually will help the client realize his or her accomplishments and vision for the future.

DECISION MAKING

A variety of decision-making conditions exist for recreation specialists. Decision theorists have identified three general circumstances for the decision maker: certainty, risk, and uncertainty (Huber, 1980).

Certainty

In theory, certainty means that a manager, when faced with a decision, knows the exact outcome of each alternative that is being considered. In reality, when managers have to make a decision, absolute certainty never exists.

Risk

A more common decision-making condition is a state of risk. Essentially a state of risk implies that the manager knows the probabilities associated with the possible outcomes of the alternative under consideration. The probability may be based on statistical or recorded experiences, or on subjective judgment. Subjective probability estimates are the product of the manager's experience and judgment. In decision making under conditions of risk the level of risk is moderate. However, the ability to recognize and take a calculated risk is a skill required of all managers.

Uncertainty

The final condition is uncertainty. In this situation, the manager does not know all of the alternatives, the risks associated with each, or the consequences each alternative is likely to have. This condition is the most ambiguous for managers. According to Ayert and De Groot (1984), the key to effective decision making under the condition of uncertainty is to acquire as much relevant information as possible and to approach the situation from a logical and rational perspective. Intuition, judgment, and experience play a major role in this condition as well.

Certainty, risk, and uncertainty may be viewed as a conceptual continuum that helps managers visualize and think about the decisions that face them. Although therapeutic recreation managers face decisions every day, they are more inclined to make decisions that fall between certainty and risk (O'Morrow & Carter, 1997, pp. 148-149).

Managers are not the only individuals that make decisions. The participant often knows his or her abilities and limitations. Ultimately, the decision maker is the participant. A participant must be open and frank regarding limitations and weigh the decision based on the risk factors and the need to experience the activity. Decisions by the participant are also determined by the age, maturity level, and skill demonstrated in similar activities that carry the same demand or ability.

ACTIVITY ANALYSIS, MODIFICATION, AND OUTDOOR THERAPEUTIC RECREATION ACTIVITIES

Successful involvement in some outdoor therapeutic recreation activities may initially appear unrealistic for individuals with certain disabilities. The activity analysis process breaks down activities into the basic behavioral requirements necessary for successful participation. Stumbo and Peterson (2002) suggested that activities be divided into physical, cognitive, affective, and social requirements. Physical requirements include outdoor therapeutic recreation activities that include sitting, standing, kneeling, etc. The amount of flexibility, types of movement, endurance needed, speed, strength, and coordination required are all considerations. Affective requirements include the intensity of emotions that may be expressed and the range of emotions that may be required. Cognitive requirements include concentration, level of planning, strategy, and memory retention. Social requirements include the relationship skills that are needed to work and play with others during the outdoor therapeutic recreation activity. The following protocols identify the requirements that may or may not match the individual's ability. Through modification and adaptation, the participant's personal skills may be able to reach the requirements for at least entry level into the program and activity. (Howe-Murphy & Charboneau, 1987)

Extensive modification of an activity can sometimes take the fun and purpose out of the activity. The activity's meaning is reduced. A sound rule of thumb: if the activity is not recognizable based on the original design, then its value, fun, and purpose may be diminished.

GENERAL CONSIDERATIONS FOR MODIFYING ACTIVITIES

The following list of general considerations for modifying activities is extremely helpful in the design, development, implementation, and evaluation stages. The list is also crucial to the sound organization of the protocol for each activity offered for and with the client.

Individuals need to recognize, identify, and relate to the activity offered. It is important to make sure the action is ongoing and it provides the participant with a level of satisfaction that is desirable.

Rules, regulations, and procedures should remain as constant as possible to preserve the integrity of the action. Remember, we are working *with individuals* — individually, in small or large groups.

Assuming modifications must be used is often a mistake. Persons with disabilities more often than not can participate without any noticeable adaptations or modifications.

Success is extremely important. Jay B. Nash, a pioneer in physical education and recreation, believed in the right and need of all individuals to belong. In order to belong, one must have a degree of success. An activity or program must be evaluated and reevaluated to constantly provide the greatest benefit to the participant. Analyzing activities and then choosing those experiences that meet the biopsychosocial demands and wishes of the client is the primary goal of any quality activity and program.

Keep the activity in action as close to the original activity as possible (Stumbo & Peterson, 2002).

1. Modify only the rules, transportation, and equipment that need adapting to allow the individual's participation at the highest level.
2. Individualize or modify to the individual's needs and desires.
3. Do not assume that the activity needs to be modified or adapted.
4. When a client succeeds, consider changing the activity to a higher level.
5. If the client is not succeeding, consider another activity analysis to determine a success level.
6. Reevaluate the activity to improve its effectiveness for the individual and group.

ADAPTATIONS

Being able to adapt to one's environment is the primary goal of all animals. Human beings, like all living things, naturally adapt to the dynamic situations of life.

Three basic forms of adaptations exist (Bullock & Mahon, 1999; p. 247)

1. *Find, create, or modify equipment* or add an assistive device that allows a person to accomplish a skill or compensate for lack of a capability.

2. *Change the method* by which the individual accomplishes or performs a skill.

3. *Change the rules or procedures* to allow modification of the lacking skill, elimination of that skill or capability as a necessity for participation, or the addition of an alternative skill for all participants involved in the activity.

In programming, I believe in the approach that I term the BBS System. In essence, these three letters stand for a philosophy that provides the greatest benefit to all clients and provides the least monetary expenditures. The first B stands for Beg. We must carefully and diligently request the support of the private sector (e.g., factories, businesses, and churches) and the public sector (e.g., schools, parks and recreation agencies, colleges, and universities) to provide software, hardware, and monetary contributions.

When contributions are not available, the second B comes into action: borrow. Historically, our ancestors used a barter system. This system of sharing goods provided the necessary means to have quality products and items to provide the service. Recreation providers must develop and foster better community and private relationships.

The S equals, in the kindest sense the word, steal. We must seek every opportunity to utilize free, leftover, and thrown away items for our programs. Many businesses and factories discard items designed for one purpose that can be used by Therapeutic Recreation and Outdoor Recreation Specialists for another purpose. Thus, the BBS system should be a philosophy that provides the spark to develop new creative programs.

THERAPEUTIC RECREATION/OUTDOOR RECREATION ACTIVITY LEADERSHIP MODEL

Dr. Ronald Packard, a park and recreation professional and my colleague in the early years of recreation education, discussed the concept of recreation activity leadership with all the students at Post College in Waterbury, Connecticut. Snyder's Therapeutic Recreation/-Outdoor Recreation Activity Leadership model is a modified version of this concept.

Life is full of activities with various goals, objectives, and processes. The Therapeutic Recreation/Outdoor Recreation Activity Leadership Model is a structured means to effectively engage, motivate, activate, and educate the participant. Re-creating the activity and doing the activity again improves the participant's skill. This is how we learn and grow.

How many times have we not wanted to participate because of fear of lecturing from the leader or the belief that the rules or procedures are too difficult or complex? There are three basic steps in teaching an activity. As the chart on the next page shows, they are motivation, activation, and education.

Motivation is a process of getting the individual into the action quickly and keeping enthusiasm by changing the action to meet the needs of the individuals in the group. Remember, we cannot start a car until we

THREE BASIC STEPS TO EFFECTIVE THERAPEUTIC RECREATION TEACHING AND LEARNING

I	II	III
MOTIVATION Get the participants interested through your own enthusiasm.	**ACTIVATION** Let them play the game as quickly as possible.	**EDUCATION** Answer questions and teach the more complicated rules and activity strategies as they play and learn. Revisit the activity regarding skills and lessons learned.

provide oil, oxygen, water, fuel, and spark. Motivation is providing basic ingredients in the activity; the spark that leads us into the activation stage.

Activation is just like the cylinders in a vehicle. Remember, we cannot tune up a car until we get it going. So start the activity as soon as you possibly can. Don't worry about explaining all the details first. That's the part that really isn't all that much fun.

The activation stage is broken down into even more parts. They include formation, explanation, demonstration, modification and adaptation, re-explanation, and play. The figure on the next page shows the flow of the process.

Start by getting the participants in the *formation* that is most efficient. The *explanation* stage is equal to our vehicle owner's manual. It provides who, what, when, where, why, and how regarding the activity.

THE ACTIVATION PHASE

FORMATION
Get your participants into the formation the game requires.

EXPLANATION
"The object of this game is…"

DEMONSTRATION
"This is the way you should try to do it…"

MODIFICATION & ADAPTATIONS
"What is the most efficient and enjoyable way…"

RE-EXPLAIN
Show and tell at the same time to reinforce learning.

PLAY
Provide the activity.

A good activity leader is like a good salesperson. We need to sell the activity with a *demonstration* of its effectiveness and worthiness.

No automobile is designed for any one person. We do *modifications and adaptations* to our seating, steering wheel height, mirrors, and other components in order to be safe and comfortable. All activities that we do in life are modified daily, consciously and unconsciously. This is true even in our activities of daily living (ADL). Some individuals shave first in the morning, others brush their teeth. We must constantly ask ourselves, "What is the most efficient way that I can accomplish this task?"

Driving a motor vehicle is a skill that is learned through a process of teaching, performing, teaching, and redoing. When we find a concern, we *re-explain* the game. We need to show and tell at the same time to reinforce what is learned. One can be told how to ride a bike. It is not until you are shown, assisted, fail, and restart that you succeed.

Play is the essence of our life. I believe that "Recreation is my therapy." The process of doing what we want and need to do at a time chosen by us is the essence of fulfillment in our life. Play is a means of providing an activity that meets our biopsychosocial needs.

Education, the third basic step, can be formal and informal. It can be in a four-walled environment or in the open outdoors. Recreation is education at the highest level by providing fun, enjoyment, skills, knowledge, processes, and techniques in the most conducive, pleasurable environment of learning and re-learning. Recreation is the education activity of the leisure environment. We need to answer questions at the time they are asked by our participants to encourage interest and to show a caring attitude toward the activity. Education is like automobile design. We must provide the basics and then provide the complexities to contribute to our wants and needs. Aristotle, the Greek philosopher, would remind us that Form follows Function. The primary duty of education is providing the skills necessary, the form, to make the function of our activity a success. The activity leader must constantly ask: What did the participant enjoy? How and what did they learn?

EFFECTIVE RECREATION

Leadership and programming are essential in providing quality recreation programs. These skills are something all of us should strive for.

Three basic qualities of an effective leader for inclusive therapeutic recreation and outdoor recreation activities:

1. Has an abundance of enthusiasm.
2. Finds joy in working with people.
3. Knows a variety of games and activities and how to teach them.

Four basic steps of effective programming in outdoor/therapeutic recreation:

1. Select activities to meet the needs, interests, and abilities of people.
2. Arrange the activities logically so that they are easy to organize and lead.
3. Prepare materials and equipment beforehand.
4. Program with and not for people.

SNYDER'S FIVE-POINT DIAGRAM

Snyder's five-point diagram for modification and adaptation of activities for persons with disabilities allows the therapist to consider all of the important aspects of a program for a particular population. This diagram can be an excellent check-and-balance for providing quality outdoor therapeutic recreation experiences to meet the needs and interests of the individual. Professionals and volunteers using this diagram need to take into account the following five factors as shown on the following page:

- Program Activity
- Facility
- Equipment
- Transportation
- Staff

There are specific considerations that need to be addressed for each of the areas during program planning:

1.   PROGRAM ACTIVITY
    - number of clients attending
    - age and gender
    - physical, cognitive, and social interaction skill levels for participation
    - ability (how well clients use skills)
    - health status (temporary or permanent)
    - knowledge of activity
    - disability (temporary or permanent)
    - activity itself (does activity require modification?)
    - safety and risk management plan

SNYDER'S FIVE-POINT DIAGRAM FOR MODIFYING PROGRAMS AND ACTIVITIES

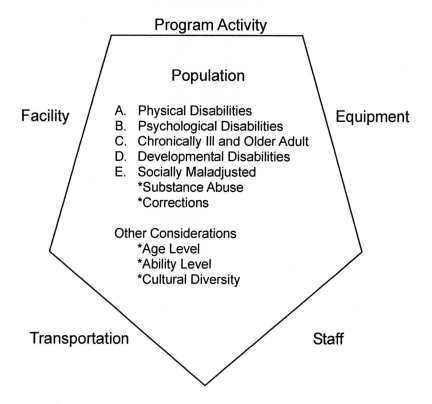

Program Activity

Facility

Equipment

Population

A. Physical Disabilities
B. Psychological Disabilities
C. Chronically Ill and Older Adult
D. Developmental Disabilities
E. Socially Maladjusted
   *Substance Abuse
   *Corrections

Other Considerations
   *Age Level
   *Ability Level
   *Cultural Diversity

Transportation

Staff

2.   FACILITY
- availability; enough space
- location
- accessibility
- cost
- appearance
- repair and maintenance
- sanitary conditions
- accessibility of rest rooms
- safety and risk management plan

3.   EQUIPMENT
- available or need to purchase
- modifications or other equipment used
- repair and maintenance, safety

4.   TRANSPORTATION
- to and from the facility; driving time
- how many clients and how many (wheelchair) vans needed
- will transportation stay or leave during program
- safety and risk management plan

5.   STAFF
- full-time, part-time, volunteers, students
- staff to client ratio
- skills and abilities of staff (e.g., professionals or volunteers)
- certifications and training required
- staff member job descriptions and responsibilities
- supervision
- leadership
- safety and risk management plan

All programs should meet the needs and interests of the individuals. Safety should be a primary concern of the facilitator and the participant.

It is very important to address all of these areas in order to have a sound and complete program and activity. Any good outdoor/therapeutic recreation program utilizes adaptations at some time and in some form to maximize an individual's success and to compensate for his or her limitations. Each one of the five factors must be examined in detail. This examination is best done through brainstorming or using a formal method of analysis like the Phillips 66 Method.

The Phillips 66 Method was developed by Donald J. Phillips who found that using six people to examine an issue for six minutes produced numerous ideas in a very structured and timesaving manner. One individual should take notes and list ideas, activities, suggestions, or solutions that can be developed by the group in a timely manner by focusing on each of the five factors and the specific population.

The above areas and needs can be used as a checklist for preparation for implementation of any activity. Formal and informal, formative and summative evaluation is a key for quality assurance.

BARRIERS TO PARTICIPATION

McIntonsh and Goeldner (1984), Epperson (1977), and others have offered the following barriers to travel and to recreation in general:

Expense is typically given as one of the top two barriers. This is particularly a problem with low-income groups, large families, and senior citizens on fixed incomes.

Lack of Time is the second of the two most common barriers. Business-persons and other professionals typically offer this as a barrier to their participation.

Physical Condition, depending upon the activity, can be a significant barrier to persons with disabilities or health problems.

Family Status limits participation by adults and families with small children. Recently, the large number of single women with children has been observed as a related trend.

Lack of Interest is a barrier that affects everyone for one recreation pursuit or another. However, some people say they have a lack of interest when another barrier is actually the real problem.

Lack of Skills restricts many people from attempting an activity they might otherwise enjoy.

Lack of Companions, particularly for travel, is a significant barrier for some single people and many senior citizens.

Lack of Knowledge about what is available is a surprising but common barrier in our complex society.

Lack of Safety, whether traveling in foreign countries or in your own hometown, will deter people from participation. Even if safety is no longer a problem in a given area, the negative perception and reputation of an area might linger for years.

Lack of Transportation, particularly for day-to-day recreation purposes, is a barrier to urban and rural people alike. If people have the financial resources and plan properly, this should not be a problem unless there is a deficiency in the transportation network.

Cyndi Chamberland, Massachusetts Department of Conservation and Recreation consultant, states that lack of experience and lack of support are common barriers to persons with disabilities and their success in programs and services. Barriers are defined in this document as external blocks to participation and success. Problems are internal limitations of the participant that include health status and emotional, physical, cognitive, and social limitations. Donald R. Snyder, Professor and Graduate Coordinator at Springfield College, has observed that time and money are the most common excuses for non-participation.

Chapter Three

Activity Protocols

Donald R. Snyder
Marcy Marchello
Angela M. Cullinan
Anne Rothshadl
Cyndy Chamberland
Robert Accorsi

Introduction

The following list of programs includes organized activities that take place in Massachusetts' state forests and parks. These activities have been facilitated as free weekly individual programs and as open house events in which multiple activities may take place in one park. Conventional state park activities such as picnicking, walking, and swimming are not included here, as these are usually doable by most people independently once the site has been improved for accessibility. By providing equipment, leadership, instruction, safety, adaptations, and support for more complex activities, DCR has helped open the doors to outdoor recreation at a local level for people with disabilities who might otherwise never have experienced the joys of paddling through water lilies or gliding across a snowy landscape.

Remember that in choosing sites for accessible recreation programs, it is essential that the sites offer accessible parking and restrooms. Another very important consideration is the availability of public transportation. While many people with disabilities may drive and own their own vehicles, many others do not drive and may be dependent upon public transportation or family for rides. Sites that are on public transportation routes are the most accessible and will allow more independence for people coming to a program on their own. In some cases, special transportation arrangements may need to be made to make the program truly accessible for people with transportation limitations.

At regularly occurring programs, pre-registration is often required so that participants may be scheduled for an introductory lesson or a supported recreational experience. The pre-registration process also allows for staff to get familiar with who will be attending, what adaptations they might require, and ensure that everyone will have appropriate equipment available. As equipment quantity and sizes may be limited, pre-registration is an important aspect of setting up a successful program. Personal goals, appropriate clothing, special needs, as well as other information can be collected and discussed in advance in order to better prepare participants and staff for a successful experience.

Larger events are considered open to the public. Advertising takes place through the DCR website, mailings, press releases, posters, and phone calls to known participants for all programs and events. In all cases, the Universal Access Program and Shared Ventures Outdoors

Grant Project have served people of all ages, as individuals, families, and groups, at little to no cost for participants.

The programs are intended to be a starting point for people with disabilities to gain basic knowledge, skills, and experience in a given activity. Those who want to continue to pursue the activity at a more advanced level will do so of their own accord, either independently or through other recreation organizations. Exposure to the park system through adaptive programs invites participants with disabilities to visit parks on their own as well. The programs are also intended to create an environment in which people with more severe disabilities may attend as many times as they wish in order to make use of the instruction, assistance, adaptations, safety, and equipment that provide a stable structure for recreation.

The following activity protocols offer a baseline of information for either starting an adaptive recreation program or integrating people with disabilities into existing recreation programs. These activity protocols are designed to be useful for general planning and as a starting point for protocols that are modified to meet the needs of programs being developed by the readers of this text. It is standard for all protocols to be signed and dated in conjunction with the development of programs. Be mindful of the biopsychosocial demands and requirements of each activity as it is broken down into smaller components of accomplishment. These are not outlined in the following protocols but are standard in therapeutic recreation practice. All protocols should have formative and summative evaluations.

Alphabetical Order

- Camping
- Cross-Country Skiing
- Cycling
- Fishing
- Hiking
- Ice-skating
- Nature Photography
- Nature Walks
- Flatwater Paddling (Canoeing and Kayaking)
- Rowing
- Snowmobiling

Seasonal Order

Winter Season Programs
- Cross-Country Skiing
- Ice-skating
- Snowmobiling

Spring, Summer, and Fall Season Programs
- Camping
- Cycling
- Fishing
- Hiking
- Nature Walks
- Flatwater Paddling (Canoeing and Kayaking)
- Rowing

All Seasons
- Nature Photography

Outline of Protocol

Program Title

General Purpose

Outcomes Desired

Description of the Program

Facilities

Staff

Equipment

Variations

Addressable Problems

Facilities

Equipment

Participants

Special Considerations

Recreation Techniques

General

Adaptive

Risk Management

Program Evaluation

Additional Notes

Winter Season Programs

- **Cross-Country Skiing**

- **Ice-Skating**

- **Snowmobiling**

Cross-Country Skiing

Angela M. Cullinan

Megan Briggs sit-skiing through Wendell State Forest.

General Purpose

To provide accessible cross-country skiing opportunities for persons who require adapted equipment, instruction, and assistance.

Outcomes Desired

- Knowledge and skills to cross-country ski as independently as possible
- Opportunity for inclusive socialization
- Experience the natural outdoor winter environment
- A challenging, aerobic activity to increase individuals' physical health

Description of the Program

Facilities

An outdoor cross-country skiing park or facility is necessary. Snow conditions should be appropriate to run program. Ideal temperatures are above 20°F. Avoid dangerous weather such as significant snowstorms. Avoid icy conditions for new or vulnerable skiers. Be able to contact everyone in case of a cancellation.

Staff

Three to twenty staff people (skilled volunteers are acceptable as additional staff people). Enough trained staff and volunteers should be on hand to assist with the program, including transferring participants to and from sit-skis; with some staff remaining at base and others assisting on the trail. Three staff should have current first aid and CPR certifications. All staff members must be proficient cross-country skiers and have had disability etiquette and awareness training.

Staffing ratios with the skiers should be one-on-one or two-on-one depending on the skier's ability:
- One-on-one for physically fit, skilled skiers (both sit-skiing and stand-skiing).
- Two-on-one when support work is required to handle terrain for weaker, less skilled skiers (volunteers in training can be added to ski parties).

Program leaders and volunteers should be knowledgeable about the following sit-ski techniques for both one-on-one ratio and two-on-one ratio and be able to teach and assist:
- Sizing people and sit-skis for best fit and safety.
- Forward ski techniques for sit-skiers.
- Backward ski technique for sit-skiers.
- Turning techniques for sit-skiers.
- Braking techniques for sit-skiers.
- Tethering techniques for stand-skiers to assist sit-skiers by pulling and braking as needed.
- How to safely return to upright position after falling — for all skiers.
- Sighted guide ski techniques for stand-skiers to assist visually impaired stand-skiers.
- Snowshoeing techniques for those who are able to walk and prefer not to ski.

Equipment
- Six or more cross-country sit-skis (various sizes including children and adult) and cross-country sit-ski poles.

- Twelve sets of cross-country skis (various sizes including children and adults, snowshoes can be substituted for cross-country skis), ski boots, and ski poles in various sizes.
- Skis: waxed, adjustments made, poles checked, and working properly before program. All necessary straps should be on each sit-ski.
- Waist packs should contain a set of shock-corded webbing, first aid supplies, power bar, hand warming packet, ski wax, and a map of the park.
- A box of adaptive supplies including foam bolsters, duct tape, Velcro strips, stools, and straps.
- Inform participant to wear proper clothing for winter conditions, including extra hats, mittens, scarves, fleeces, socks, etc. Encourage participants to bring a change of clothes for when they are done skiing.

Variations

- Small group of staff (one to three) ski with a single skier with a disability in a small, customized ski experience or lesson.
- Public attends ski program or other winter event at park.

Addressable Problems

Facilities

Facility access

Facilities used should be fully accessible to provide the best experience. If they are not, the following adaptations may be made. However, the adaptations are not optimum solutions and should not be presented as such.

- Temporary ramps may be installed to provide access up one step into building, restrooms, or warming hut.

- Mats may be installed outside to provide a solid surface to maneuver wheelchairs or crutches over snow.
- Side entrances may be used to access building or warming hut.
- Accessible Port-A-Potties may be rented if inside bathrooms are not accessible or building is closed for the season.
- Additional personal assistance may be required in bathroom, with ADLs (activities of daily living), etc.

Facilities not plowed
- Parking lots, sidewalks, and park roads should be plowed in advance of the program.

Trails not groomed
- Program leaders should contact park supervisors prior to the program day to inform them of areas that will need to be groomed.

Program is too far and not accessible by public transportation
- Provide cross-country skiing experiences or winter outdoor recreation experiences in a park where public transportation is accessible.
- Help facilitate ride sharing and transportation arrangements as needed.

Equipment
- Have clothing available if it is required.

Participants
Participants who have visual impairments will be better able to navigate and enjoy skiing with a sighted guide. Participants with mobility or endurance difficulties should be assisted on an as needed basis.

Special Considerations

- mobility impairments
- vulnerability to cold temperatures
- seizure conditions
- disabilities affecting verbal and non-verbal communication
- poor balance
- brittle bones
- circulatory conditions
- sighted guides
- limited upper body strength
- hemiplegia

Recreation Techniques

General

- Participants should be prepared and dressed for cold outdoor weather conditions.
- Everyone should be formally introduced to the equipment; include the dangers of not following directions when cross-country skiing.
- Trail maps should be provided so all participants have an idea of where they will be skiing.

Adaptive

- Provide foam, bungee straps, chest straps, and other adaptive equipment so participants are fitted to the sit-ski appropriately. Extra clothing can also be tucked around the skier for support as needed.
- Persons with limited mobility, including upper and lower body

strength should have the following adaptations:

- o Chest strap should be comfortably fitted around participant's chest. High back ski frame required for this modification.
- o Foam should be used for extra support under knees, behind lower back, etc.
- o Stand-skier should tether in to provide pulling, steering, and braking support as needed.
- o Participants should be comfortable falling sideways — deep soft snow conditions at trailside are preferred. Avoid icy conditions. Helmet may be advisable.

- Transfer assistance should be available both onto and off of sit-ski (if needed).
- Shorten route if participant is uncomfortable, fatigued, or if weather has changed.
- Allow persons with visual impairments to touch skis and snowshoes. Guide hands while explaining different parts on skis and snowshoes.
- Provide assistive listening devices as needed. The instructor wears a transmitter. The participant wears a receiver that can adjust the volume of the instructor's voice. This is great for people who are hard of hearing, people who fall to the rear of the group while traveling, and kids who need a way to focus.

Risk Management

- Have enough park and trail maps on hand for everyone.
- Know and follow the emergency management plan of the park.
- Maintain ski equipment.
- Have participants, staff, and volunteers sign waiver forms prior to skiing.
- Know and have ready access to the person on duty at the park.

- Minimize risky behavior by being aware of what is going on in the program.
- Provide a warming area.
- Avoid frigid temperatures and dangerous weather.
- Provide warm drinks, snacks, and extra clothing for outdoor programs or have participants bring them.
- Carry radios or other communication devices on the trail. (Cell phones will not work in all areas.)
- Be aware of signs of hypothermia and frostbite and know how to prevent and treat them.

Program Evaluation

Session reports:
1. Instructors fill out report, one page per session
2. Instructors do a seasonal report including recommendations for future improvements
3. Accessibility survey
4. Record of participant comments during the program
5. Informal post-event interview of participants
6. Analysis of survey and comments

Management evaluation:
1. Assessing incoming information
2. Making adjustments (publicity, equipment, scheduling)

Additional Notes

From our experience the best time to run this program is January-March.

Ice-Skating

Angela M. Cullinan

Ice-sledding is part of the Massachusetts' Department of Conservation and Recreation program.

General Purpose

To provide accessible ice-skating for people who require accessible equipment, instruction, and assistance.

Outcomes Desired

- Knowledge and skills to skate as independently as possible
- Opportunity for inclusive socialization
- Opportunity to experience and enjoy ice-skating in an indoor ice rink or a frozen outdoor pond

Description of the Program

Facilities

Ice-skating can be done either at an indoor rink or in a state park where ponds are frozen. Outdoor ponds must have six inches of ice for the pond to be deemed safe and skating must by approved by a park supervisor for the day.

Conditions should be appropriate to run an outdoor ice-skating program. Ideal temperatures are above 20°F. There should be an accessible warming area.

Staff

A minimum of two staff are necessary. Enough staff should be on hand to accommodate the number of people attending. Pre-registration for the program helps prepare staff.

People leading ice-skating programs should be knowledgeable about ice sleds and adaptations. They should have some basic disability awareness and etiquette training, first aid, and CPR.

Equipment

- Three to six ice sleds, one should have a high seat back to provide upper body support.
- One set of ice sticks (for right and left hand) per sled, one set of ice sticks should have hand adaptation for persons with poor fine motor skills in hands.
- An adaptive supply kit with foam bolsters, duct tape, Velcro strips, and Velcro chest straps.
- Park radio to contact park personnel (for outdoor programs).
- Hockey puck(s) and goal, or parking cones to create goal.
- Stroller bar that can be inserted into ice sleds to push participant in sled.
- Ice walker: a walker with short skis mounted at the bottom for sliding and walking with stability on ice, snow covered ice, or snow to ice.
- Participants should wear warm clothing (hats, gloves, coats, etc.) for outdoor and indoor programs.

Variations

- Public skate time, indoor rinks, one-two hours
- Private skate time, indoor rinks, one-two hours
- Outdoor program, outdoor pond, two-five hours

Addressable Problems

Facilities

Facility access

Facilities used should be fully accessible to provide the best experience. If they are not, the following adaptations may be made. However, the adaptations are not optimum solutions and should not be presented as such.

- Temporary ramps may be installed to provide access up one step into building, restrooms, or warming hut.
- Mats may be installed outside to provide a solid surface to maneuver wheelchairs or crutches over snow.
- Side entrances may be used to access building or warming hut.
- Accessible Port-A-Potties may be rented if inside bathrooms are not accessible or building is closed for the season.
- Additional personal assistance may be required in bathroom, with ADLs (activities of daily living), etc.

Facilities not plowed

Parking lots, sidewalks, and park roads should be plowed in advance of the program.

Program is too far and not accessible by public transportation

Provide a rink or outdoor ice-skating experience in a park where public transportation is accessible.

Prohibitive fees to enter rinks and rent skates

Ice skate rental fees and rink use fees may be too high for many people to afford, especially large families or groups. Ice-skating sleds can be provided for free use, and a discount fee structure could be implemented, such as a $15 cap for families.

Over-crowded rinks

Ice sled participants may be in potential danger if rinks are over-crowded. Rink management is likely to want the final say as to whether the rink is too crowded for seated skaters to skate safely for liability reasons. Best scenarios for seated skating are when the rink is relatively quiet, as in public skating hours during the week, or when or if the rink time can be exclusive for accessible ice-skating and not open to the whole public.

Equipment

Ice sleds should be thoroughly checked before the program to be sure there are no loose parts and seatbelts and straps are intact and functional. Blades should be sharpened periodically. Nuts and bolts should be tight.

Participants can wear safely helmets, orange vests, face shields, hockey gloves, etc. to minimize injury from other skaters or for playing hockey.

Participants

Participants who have visual impairments will be better able to navigate and enjoy ice-skating with a sighted guide. Participants with mobility or endurance difficulties should be assisted on an as needed basis.

Special Considerations

- Sensitivity to loud noises and bright lights
- Mobility impairments
- Vulnerability to cold temperatures
- Seizure conditions

- Disabilities affecting verbal and non-verbal communication
- Disruptive behavior
- Poor balance
- Hemiplegia

Recreation Techniques

General

- Participants should be prepared and dressed for cold indoor and outdoor weather conditions.
- Everyone should be formally introduced to the equipment.

Adaptive

- Provide foam, Velcro straps, and other adaptive equipment so participants are fitted comfortably in their ice sleds.
- A mat should be laid out (if needed) to allow participants who use crutches or wheelchairs easy access to ice.
- Persons with limited mobility, including minimal upper and lower body strength should have the following adaptations:
  - o Velcro chest strap should be comfortably fitted around participant's chest; ice sled should have a high back to accommodate adaptation.
  - o Foam should be placed behind back, or under legs to provide extra support and warmth.
  - o Hand adaptations should be provided for persons with poor fine motor skills. Sticks can be outfitted with handles for holding hands in place. (These can be made of bicycle inner tubes bolted to the stick, with Fastex (or other brand) buckle for easy opening and adjusting tension of handle).
- Transfer assistance should be provided both onto and off of ice as needed.

- Allow persons with visual impairments to touch ice sleds. Guide hands while explaining different parts on ice sled.
- Ice hockey programs can be implemented during private ice time or outdoors. Many people will find skating more appealing when a game is part of the experience.
- Many people who do not have mobility impairments will appreciate using the sleds because they have other conditions or disabilities that make seated skating much safer or more comfortable for them.

Risk Management

- Be prepared for the weather.
- For disability groups: make sure enough staff and equipment is available to meet individual needs and to monitor individual behavior and communication.
- Have participants, staff, and volunteers sign waiver forms prior to ice-skating.
- Know and follow emergency management procedures of the park or rink.
- Know and have ready access to the person on duty at the facility.
- Be aware of what's going on in the program, including levels of risk.
- Staff should be covered by insurance.
- Ice conditions should be appropriate for safe ice-skating.
- Avoid frigid temperatures.
- Provide a warming area for outside program.
- Helmets should be worn by vulnerable participants.
- Follow incident protocol.

Program Evaluation

Session reports:

1. Instructors fill out report, one page per session
2. Instructors do a seasonal report including recommendations for future improvements
3. Accessibility survey
4. Record of participant comments during the program
5. Informal post-event interview of participants
6. Analysis of survey and comments

Management evaluation:

1. Assessing incoming information
2. Making adjustments (publicity, equipment, scheduling)

Additional Notes

This program may be run while other outdoor winter activities are happening. From our experience the best time to run this program is January-March.

Snowmobiling

Angela M. Cullinan

Snowmobiling in a Massachusetts State Forest.

General Purpose

To provide accessible snowmobiling opportunities for persons who require adaptations and assistance.

Outcomes Desired

- Experience of a snowmobile ride
- A winter recreation experience that is accessible, using motorized transportation
- Opportunity for inclusive socialization

Description of the Program

Facilities

The ideal facility would be a park where snowmobiling is allowed and where shorter trips (thirty minutes to one hour per ride) are logical and fun. Snow conditions should be appropriate to run program. Ideal temperatures are above 20°F. Avoid dangerous weather such as significant snowstorms. Be able to contact everyone in case of a cancellation.

Staff

Minimum of two staff (paid or volunteer) who are knowledgeable about proper adaptations, operation of a snowmobile, first aid, CPR, and who have disability and awareness training. Persons operating snowmobiles should be of legal age and have appropriate driver's license. Persons driving snowmobile should have some basic disability and etiquette training. Enough trained staff should be on hand to assist with the program, including transferring participants to and from snowmobiles as needed.

Equipment

- Snowmobiles should be working properly before the program, gas tanks should be filled, brakes should be checked, and snowmobiles should be registered in the state in which they are operating.
- The program should require all participants to wear helmets. (Not all states require snowmobile riders to wear helmets.)
- The program should have at least one snowmobile that provides upper body support, backrest, or Velcro chest strap.
- Adaptive supply kit with foam bolsters, duct tape, Velcro strips, and bungee cords is recommended.
- Park radio to contact park personnel.
- Roll out mats.

Variations

- Snowmobiles and drivers provided by facility
- Snowmobiles and drivers provided by snowmobile club

Addressable Problems

Facilities

Facility access

Facilities used should be fully accessible to provide the best experience. If they are not, the following adaptations may be made. However, the adaptations are not optimum solutions and should not be presented as such.

- Temporary ramps may be installed to provide access up one step into building, restrooms, or warming hut.
- Mats may be installed outside to provide a solid surface to maneuver wheelchairs or crutches over snow.
- Side entrances may be used to access building or warming hut.

- Accessible Port-A-Potties may be rented if inside bathrooms are not accessible or building is closed for the season.
- Additional personal assistance may be required in bathroom, with ADLs (activities of daily living), etc.

Facilities not plowed
Parking lots, sidewalks, and park roads should be plowed in advance of the program.

Program is too far and not accessible by public transportation
Provide snowmobiling experience or winter outdoor recreation experience in a park where public transportation is accessible. Assist participants in connecting with rides or making transportation arrangements as needed.

Snowmobile trails are not groomed
Program leaders should contact park supervisors prior to program day to inform them of areas that will need to be groomed and confirm grooming arrangements to accommodate program.

Participants
Snowmobile clubs may have their own special liability requirements, which may include additional waiver forms and insurance.

Special Considerations

- Sensitivity to loud noises and exhaust fumes
- Mobility impairments
- Vulnerability to cold temperatures
- Seizure conditions
- Disabilities affecting verbal and non-verbal communication
- Disruptive behavior

Recreation Techniques

General

- Participants should be prepared and dressed for cold outdoor weather conditions.
- Everyone should be formally introduced to the equipment; include the dangers of not following directions when riding a snowmobile and warn individuals of noise and exhaust fumes.
- Trail maps should be provided so all participants have an idea of where they will be riding.

Adaptive

- Snowmobiles should be easily accessed. Instead of having snowmobiles parked in the field, have snowmobiles in the parking lot or near a shoveled walkway.
- Provide foam, bungee straps, chest straps, and other adaptive equipment so participants can be fitted to the snowmobile for a comfortable ride.
- Persons with limited mobility, including minimal upper and lower body strength, should have the following adaptations:
  - o Chest strap should be comfortably fitted around participant's chest; snowmobile should have a high back to accommodate adaptation.
  - o A bungee cord can be used to keep participants legs from falling to the side. The bungee should be placed near the foot of the participant and should be brought across to the other foot. The bungee cord should be tight enough to keep the legs in place, but should not be so tight that circulation is cut off.
  - o Foam should be placed behind the back (lumbar curve) of participant, especially if the individual needs extra support or is sitting too far away from the driver. Additional foam can

be placed where needed. Duct tape will be sufficient to hold foam in place.

- Transfer assistance should be available both onto and off of the snowmobile.
- Shorten route if participant is uncomfortable or adaptations have shifted.
- Allow persons with visual impairments to touch snowmobiles. Guide hands while explaining different parts of the snowmobile.
- Provide assistive listening devices as needed.

Risk Management

- Have enough park and trail maps on hand for everyone.
- Ride the snowmobile trail prior to program to make sure trail is properly groomed and no debris are in the way.
- Staff should have proper training before operating snowmobiles.
- Snowmobiles should be property maintained.
- Have staff and participants sign waiver forms prior to going on snowmobile.
- Know and follow emergency management procedures of facility.
- Know and have ready access to the person on duty at the facility.
- Be aware of what's going on in the program including levels of risk.
- Staff should be covered by insurance.
- Snow conditions should be appropriate for snowmobiling.
- Avoid frigid temperatures.
- Provide warming area.
- Participants should bring warm drinks, snacks, and extra clothing for outdoor programs.
- Follow incident report protocol.

Program Evaluation

Session reports:
1. Instructors fill out report, one page per session
2. Instructors do a seasonal report including recommendations for future improvements
3. Accessibility survey
4. Record of participant comments during the program
5. Informal post-event interview of participants
6. Analysis of survey and comments

Management evaluation:
1. Assessing incoming information
2. Making adjustments (publicity, equipment, scheduling)

Additional Notes

This program may be run while other winter activities are happening. From our experience the best time to run this program is January-March.

Spring, Summer, and Fall Seasons Programs

- **Camping**

- **Cycling**

- **Fishing**

- **Hiking**

- **Nature Walks**

- **Flatwater Paddling (Canoeing and Kayaking)**

- **Rowing**

Camping

Angela M. Cullinan

Doucett family vacations in a ramped yurt site at Nickerson State Park on Cape Cod.

General Purpose

To provide accessible camping opportunities for persons who require adaptations and assistance.

Outcomes Desired

- Knowledge and skills to camp as independently as possible
- Opportunity for inclusive socialization
- Opportunities for direct exploration of natural habitats

Description of the Program

Facilities

Campsites should have smooth, relatively hard-packed surfaces with minimal rocks, roots from trees, or debris. Campsites should also offer a raised grill and accessible (extended) picnic table.

Campsites, cabins, and yurts should be reserved several months in advanced to guarantee availability.

Staff

Enough trained staff should be on hand to assist with the program. People leading camping programs should have experience in leading outdoor camping experiences and be comfortable in the outdoors. At least two staff are required for one to two night camping programs. Three or more staff are required for camping programs longer than two nights. At least two staff must have current first aid and CPR certifications. Staff should also have disability and awareness training.

Equipment

- Basic tents for two to three people
- Tents that have two rooms (for four or more people) allow comfortable wheelchair access
- Camp stoves (two 2-burner Coleman stoves or equivalent)
- Coolers
- Tarps
- Ropes
- Lanterns
- Food and supplies for group meals
- Backup gear as needed to cover what participants are unable to bring

Variations

- Tent, cabin, or yurt camping.
- Individuals with disability and families participate in camping program.
- Disability group attends camping program.
- Food can be provided by either participants or program (but make sure enough food is available).
- Additional accessible recreation opportunities may be provided during the day to enhance the recreation experience for campers, such as nature walks, use of beach wheelchairs, adaptive cycling, hiking, fishing, paddling programs, etc.

Addressable Problems

Facilities

Facility access

Facilities used should be fully accessible to provide the best experience. If they are not, the following adaptations may be made.

However, the adaptations are not optimum solutions and should not be presented as such.

- Temporary ramps may be installed to provide access up one step into cabin, other buildings, or restrooms.
- Side entrances may be used to access building.
- Accessible Port-A-Potties may be rented if inside bathrooms are not accessible.
- Additional personal assistance may be required in bathroom, with ADLs (activities of daily living), etc.

Program is too far and not accessible by public transportation
- Provide camping experiences in a park where public transportation is accessible.
- Help facilitate ride sharing and transportation arrangements as needed.

Equipment

Not all parks have accessible cabins or yurts. Tents, camp stoves, lanterns should be working properly before program and extra fuel should be available for camp stoves. Persons with disabilities should be outfitted with the best type of equipment that meets their needs (persons in wheelchairs should be given bigger, roomier tents than persons without wheelchairs, etc.).

Special Considerations

- Mobility impairments
- Vulnerability to temperatures
- Disabilities that affect communication
- Disruptive behavior

Recreation Techniques

General

- Be prepared for outdoor conditions and encourage participants and staff to arrive prepared. Take the time in advance of the camping experience to explain what to bring to new campers.
- Communicate agenda and make sure everyone is comfortable.
- Utilize all of the senses during activities.
- Treat everyone equally.
- Encourage independence: people doing appropriate tasks by themselves, taking time on their own to explore park, sightsee in the area, etc.
- Provide routes to get to important locations such as restrooms, water supply, eating areas, and showers.

Adaptive

- Provide adaptive equipment such as foam or rope for persons who need extra support.
- Add extra padding around or under sleeping area in the tent.
- Adaptive camping equipment to suit a person's needs, such as a cot for sleeping or gel padding for seated comfort, may be used. A milk crate can be helpful as an assistive tool for anyone who needs support moving from a prone to seated or standing position on his or her own in the middle of the night.
- On-call staff person at night to assist someone if needed.
- Physical assistance for wheelchair users to help with rough terrain within the campground.
- Provide assistive listening devices, sign language, etc. as needed.
- Allow persons with visual impairments to touch camping equipment. Guide hands while explaining different parts. Assign sighted guide role to different people to assist campers with visual impairments as needed.

Risk Management

- Know who will be attending, the nature of their disabilities, special concerns, diets, etc.
- Understand the layout of the site before the participants arrive.
- Orient campers to the site including having park maps available.
- Make sure campers have access to sunscreen, bug repellent, water, etc.
- Be prepared for weather and educate campers about what this means.
- Have water, first aid kit, radio, etc. available.
- For disability groups: make sure enough staff are available to meet individual needs, monitor individual behavior, and provide necessary time for communication.
- Observe and respect camper's limits.
- Do not run program in extreme weather conditions.
- Have participants and volunteers sign waivers.
- Require staff to be covered by insurance.
- Provide food (or coordinate participants bringing food) and make sure it is stored safely.
- Have participants bring their own pillows, personal hygiene equipment, towels, etc.
- Follow incident report protocol.
- Have the means to contact the park staff quickly.

Program Evaluation

Session reports:
1. Instructors fill out report, one page per session
2. Instructors do a seasonal report including recommendations for future improvements
3. Accessibility survey

4. Record of participant comments during the program
5. Informal post-event interview of participants
6. Analysis of survey and comments

Management evaluation:
1. Assessing incoming information
2. Making adjustments (publicity, equipment, scheduling)

Additional Notes

Create a positive, inclusive, friendly atmosphere in which people of all abilities can feel part of the group and enjoy each other's company — games, music and singing, group tasks, etc. can be useful.

Cycling

Robert Accorsi

Cyndy Chamberland using a handcycle on a Massachusetts bike path.

General Purpose

To provide cycling experiences for persons who require accessible equipment, instruction, and assistance.

Outcomes Desired

- Improved cardiovascular fitness and strength
- Appreciation of outdoor recreation
- Enhancement of social, cognitive, and skill mastery abilities
- Improved overall health and wellness (holistic)
- Feelings of self-worth and self-efficacy
- Better inclusion through active involvement and skill development
- Enjoyment and fun

Description of the Program

Facilities

Facilities that are utilized must be appropriately matched to the cyclist's skill level. Attention should be given to the specific type of surfaces (asphalt, gravel, or hard-packed dirt) as it may impede the cyclist's effectiveness, thus impacting the quality of the experience.

Access to a bike shop and support from shop personnel will enhance any bike program. When a program is offered at or from a bike shop, participants have ready access to rental equipment and mechanical support. The bike shop can advertise the program and refer people to it as well.

Staff

Appropriate ratio of trained staff should be on hand to assist with the program, including transferring participants to and from the cycle if required, riding with participants on the same bike or another bike, and maintaining a presence at the base site to meet newcomers.

Participants

Select participants based on an accurate depiction of their skill level so that the skill level coincides with the route degree of difficulty.

Equipment

A multi-speed cycle coupled with proper tires for the specific terrain should provide for full utilization of the cycling route. Selection of the proper cycle is based on the specific disability. Being able to offer a range of bicycle styles and sizes is an essential foundation to meeting the needs of the variety of people likely to attend. Specialized bicycles for people with disabilities, while not commonly available in bike shops, can be found by searching the web, disability magazines, wheelchair and bicycle manufacturing companies, and sometimes even your neighborhood inventor. All cycles *must* be inspected for safety prior to riding. The following are possible bike styles:

Handcycles: Essential for people who need to use their hands and arms for pedaling, e.g., wheelchair users. Crank models are the most common, but some styles use a pumping bar. There are two main types:
1. touring model: basic starting bike, upright seated position, and
2. performance model: low rider for athletic use and speed.

Provide adult and child sizes, as well as grips especially designed for people with tetraplegia on some handcycles. Three to seven speeds keeps shifting simple for a broad user group that includes people with cognitive impairments. Twelve to 36 speeds get complicated for many people and may lead to cross-chaining problems.

Tandems: Conventional foot pedal design works well for people who have visual impairments or have balance issues. It's good to have a skilled driver who weighs at least as much as the passenger. Other tandem styles include: the Love Bike allows rear rider to steer; handcycle/footpedal combos offer options; three-wheeled tandems provide additional stability; wheelchair tandems allow for a passive rider.

Trikes: Many handcycle designs have three wheels. Footpedal trikes should also be provided, especially in adult and young adult sizes to serve senior citizens and youth. Trikes provide stability, but caution should be taken at faster speeds and on curves where these bikes can be unstable. Bike companies have designed adaptations for extra leg support and upper body support for trike riders.

Recumbent: Well known for their efficient use of body mechanics, recumbent bikes come in two and three wheel styles, and offer great potential for those who require more relaxed and centered seating, have wrist injuries or other conditions that prohibit conventional cycling posture. Some adaptive bicycle designers have built upon the recumbent style to create alternatively powered bikes, with both pedals and electric or solar assists.

Other Gear:
• Stabilizers: Training wheels or similar devices can be installed on conventional bikes to promote balance for riders who can walk.

- Adaptive supplies: foam, Velcro straps, etc.
- ANSI or Snell approved helmets in a variety of sizes
- Repair kit and air pump
- Bike gloves (personal choice)
- Bike shorts (personal choice)
- Hard-sole shoes or cycling shoes (personal choice)
- Sunglasses or other eye protectors
- Water bottles
- Maps (if available)
- Park radio (if available)

Variations

- Weekly program at base site that meets at a regular time for hourly rides or a group ride. Instruction provided on how to ride bikes as needed.
- Cycling fair with invited vendors of specialized cycling equipment and opportunities for attendees to try out bikes with instruction and support.

Addressable Problems

Facilities

Cycling routes dependant on terrain, may not be accessible for the particular skill level of the cyclist

Be sure to match the route and the participants.

Cycling routes may not be accessible by public transportation

Often times, cycling routes, trails, or paths may be located in an area not serviced by public transportation. All efforts should be made to select routes that provide the greatest participant access. When this cannot be done (as on a mountain bike trail) transportation should be provided.

Cycling routes may not be properly maintained
Program leaders must contact park supervisors prior to program day to confirm that the trail or route is suitable for cycling.

Weather
Inclement weather can occur at any time, thus causing trails and route conditions to vary and become dangerous.

Equipment

Sizing of equipment
For persons who do not own their own cycle, proper fitting is required. The individual cyclist should be fitted to the proper cycle. If a cycle doesn't fit, the individual should not be allowed to ride. A range of sizes should be available.

Maintenance
All cycles must be maintained on a regular schedule by their owners.

Helmets
All cyclists are required to wear a helmet that has passed the ANSI or SNELL safety tests. Providing additional helmets can be a good idea for groups that are not experienced cyclists. Staff should double-check that helmets are being worn properly and are correctly strapped and positioned.

Special Considerations

- Demands of cycling
- Sensitivity to heat and sun

- Endurance, strength, and flexibility
- Hydration
- Grip strength (hand cyclist)
- Asthma
- Allergies
- Visual impairments
- Balance issues
- Ability to keep limbs in position

Recreation Techniques

General

- Participants should have proper cycling clothes and be prepared for various weather conditions.
- Everyone should be properly introduced to his or her cycle (if borrowed).
- Cycling route maps should be provided.
- Check points along the route should be designated as stop areas as needed by participants. This is dependant on skill level and purpose of the ride.

Adaptive

- Persons with limited mobility, including those with trunk control difficulties should utilize:
  - o chest straps.
  - o seatbelts.
  - o pedal tie downs (clipless pedals and cycling shoes are preferred).
- Foam bolsters may be used for extra back positioning or side support — attached with duct tape.
- Power straps or Velcro straps may also be used to hold feet to

pedals. This is a better choice for two-wheeled or less stable bikes as people have the option of getting their feet out of the pedal as needed.

- Trailers or carts may be added to include younger children.
- Wheelchair using participants may be able to use their own seating pads on handcycle seats for improved comfort.
- People requiring some head support may need a head support device that can be attached to the bicycle. Staff may attempt to devise a supportive adaptation using foam, boards, tape, etc. if head support is a minor issue.
- If head support is a critical factor, it is best to provide a bike that already has a head support device built into it and not allow someone to ride until a safe support system is established.

Risk Management

- Provide trail or route maps for all riders.
- Provide sufficient supply of water or sports drinks.
- Maintain all cycles properly.
- Perform a mandatory pre-ride safety check.
- Be sure that clothing is appropriate for the conditions.
- Require a helmet to be worn at all times while on the cycle.
- Be familiar with routes.
- Have the staff covered by insurance.
- Provide waivers for participants, staff, and volunteers.
- Be sure that staff and volunteers meet the minimum skills required to assist others.
- Avoid extreme heat or cold.
- Select cycling route appropriate to skill level.
- Have enough staff and volunteers who are first aid certified.
- Have a cell phone or other communication device and

emergency numbers for services along the cycling route (be sure
that the cell phone has service on the whole route).

Program Evaluation

Session reports:
1. Instructors fill out report, one page per session
2. Instructors do a seasonal report including recommendations for
   future improvements
3. Accessibility survey
4. Record of participant comments during the program
5. Informal post-event interview of participants
6. Analysis of survey and comments

Management evaluation:
1. Assessing incoming information
2. Making adjustments (publicity, equipment, scheduling)

Additional Notes

Provide a variety of bicycle styles and plenty of staff and volunteers to
accommodate people with a wide range of characteristics in a cycling
experience.

Weather conditions are an important consideration. Avoid extremely hot
weather and dangerous storm conditions.

Fishing

Cyndy Chamberland

Even a small fish can lead to a successful fishing program.

General Purpose

To include persons of all abilities in fishing programs.

Outcomes Desired

- Knowledge and skills to fish as independently as possible
- Opportunity for inclusive socialization
- Understanding of necessary equipment, bait, license requirements, and basic fishing regulations that are needed to pursue fishing as an outdoor activity

Description of the Program

Facilities

A wide variety of places provide fishing experiences. Site used should be fully accessible with minimal grade and easy access to the fishing area.

A group-fishing permit is available at some locations. Otherwise participants and staff are required to have individual fishing licenses. Some locations have free fishing days when no licenses are required. People with physical impairments, visual impairments, mental retardation, or who are 65 and over can receive free licenses in some jurisdictions. Know your own state's license requirements.

Staff

Participants may require one-on-one for adaptive fishing. There should be a ratio of at least two staff or volunteers for every six participants. More will be required if the participants have significant disabilities or if the location presents unusual difficulties, such as fishing from boats or canoes. Staff and volunteers should be competent in fishing and have disability and awareness training. Also required:

- Instructor who understands fishing techniques, safety issues, licensing requirements, and fishing regulations.
- Staff who are trained to use adaptive equipment, first aid, CPR.
- Certified lifeguard if the participants are going out on the water.

Participants

A sign language interpreter should be brought in for anyone who is hearing impaired and communicates using sign language. Participants with behavioral problems may require special consideration.

Equipment

Fishing equipment must be suitable for the type of fishing. This protocol describes freshwater fishing, which requires equipment that is easiest to use. Equipment will be both adaptive and store bought. It includes:

- Combo fishing poles and reels (such as the ones made by Zebco) should be provided for each participant. Combo rods and reels are easy fishing equipment for beginners.
- Participants with upper extremity disabilities may require adaptive fishing equipment for casting, holding the rod or reeling. The program should have at least one Van's E-Z Cast adaptive fishing aid available that can be mounted onto a wheelchair armrest for someone with limited wrist or finger mobility, one or two strong-arm adaptive fishing aids that strap onto wrists to enable someone with limited or no grip to fish independently, and one or two Strikefighter rod holders preferably one sitting and one standing model for one-handed fishing.

- Be sure participants are wearing appropriate clothing for the conditions. Shoes or sneakers are required (no bare feet). Participants with neurological sensitivity and poor circulation are more at risk in both cold and hot conditions.
- Other fishing equipment includes a tackle box filled with extra line, hooks, sinkers, bobbers, flies, pliers, Swiss army and fishing knives, fishing net for landing fish, bucket or creel for containing catch.
- Lawn chairs or other portable chairs, preferably with back and arm supports.
- Minimum of three canoes for fishing from canoes, equipped with adaptive seating. Paddles and personal flotation devices.
- Tent for shelter from sun and rain.
- First aid kit.
- Additional equipment for ice fishing:
  - Access to an ice drill, minimum of 18 tip-ups, two to three jigs.
  - Proper bait such as a couple dozen night crawlers and mealy worms. Shiners, minnows, etc. for ice fishing.
  - Warming area.

Variations
- Freshwater fishing from shore
- Freshwater fishing from canoes
- Freshwater ice fishing
- Ocean pier fishing
- Ocean shore fishing
- Ocean charter boat fishing

Addressable Problems

Facilities

<u>Lake, pond, or river site may not be completely accessible</u>

Sand at site may be soft, muddy, or rocky inhibiting mobility. Rink matting can be placed on soft sand to maximize mobility. Accessible Port-A-Potties may be rented. Handicapped parking spots can be provided close to fishing site.

<u>Weather</u>

Be prepared for exposure to sun, rain, snow, heat, or cold (depending on when and where the event is happening).

Equipment

Be sure to have enough replacement fishing equipment for broken lines, broken hooks, or lost flies and lures.

Participants

Participants fishing from canoes may lack experience with regard to canoeing and paddling. Prior canoe experience is recommended.

Special Considerations

- Mobility impairments
- Vulnerability to temperatures and sun
- Disabilities that affect communication
- Disruptive behavior

Recreation Techniques

General

- Be prepared for outdoor conditions. Insure that participants arrive prepared. Set up a tent if possible for protection from hot sun or rain.

- Make sure everyone can see and hear instructor.
- Give the group an introduction to casting and reeling.
- Assist participants with getting fishing poles ready and baiting the hooks.
- Assist participants as needed during the program but promote participant's independence as much as possible.
- Use motivation techniques such as praising participants for casting, catching a fish, or even their patience.
- Discuss and provide information on state fishing licenses and regulations.
- Provide help with unhooking and releasing fish. (Participants may choose to bring their catch home.)
- Caution participants regarding water safety with regard to fishing from canoes or ice fishing. A certified lifeguard should go out with canoes.
- For ice fishing, drill holes for participants and give introduction to setting tip-ups and using jigs. Assist participants as needed with checking tip-ups.

Adaptive

- Provide lawn chairs for participants who have difficulty with standing or with balance.
- Assist participants as needed with set up and use of adaptive equipment.
- Provide one-on-one assistance for participants who are hearing impaired or developmentally disabled as needed.

Risk Management

- Have participants sign waiver forms prior to starting to fish.

- Have staff and volunteers fill out waivers.
- Urge participants to exercise caution regarding baiting, casting, and reeling so as not to hook themselves or one another.
- Insure that all participants, staff, and volunteers wear appropriate footwear (no bare feet).
- Require group to stay in area on shore or on lake if fishing from canoe or on ice.
- Know and follow the emergency management procedures of the facility.
- Know and have ready access to the person on duty at the facility.
- Be aware of what's going on in the program including levels of risk.
- Allow only experienced paddlers to fish from canoes.
- Require staff to be covered by insurance.
- Fish from ice only when the facility deems the conditions safe.
- Avoid frigid temperatures.
- Provide a warming (or cooling) area.
- Have participants bring cold or warm drinks and snacks.
- Follow incident report and emergency management protocols.

Program Evaluation

Session reports:
1. Instructors fill out report, one page per session
2. Instructors do a seasonal report including recommendations for future improvements
3. Accessibility survey
4. Record of participant comments during the program
5. Informal post-event interview of participants
6. Analysis of survey and comments

Management evaluation:
1. Assessing incoming information
2. Making adjustments (publicity, equipment, scheduling)

Accessible Hiking on Conventional Hiking Trails

Marcy Marchello

A wheelchair hiker usually needs a support team as grades get steeper and terrain gets rougher.

General Purpose

To include persons of all abilities on outdoor hikes on conventional hiking trails in which a group moves through one or more natural environments to experience and learn about trails, hiking techniques, and the environment.

Outcomes Desired

- Experiencing a hike as facilitated by an adaptive hiking leader in the outdoors
- Opportunities for inclusive socialization
- Hands-on participation in hiking support techniques
- Direct exploration of natural environments

Description of the Program

Facilities

Chose trails with reasonable width to accommodate participants with mobility devices and their support parties, three to four feet wide is tricky for support people if there are drop-offs. Wider trails avoid potential injury from falls for support people. Steepness and the surface of the trail should be appropriate for the group.

Staff

- People leading hikes should have expertise in hiking and backpacking. They should be skilled in using adaptive equipment with people with disabilities and have basic first aid and CPR training. Some basic disability awareness and etiquette training is also appropriate.

- Many people may be needed to provide support to participants, depending on trail difficulty and disabilities. A ratio of four to one is good for participants using a wheelchair if the trail includes steep and rugged terrain. One-on-one is good for a person with a visual impairment.
- A group of four people with disabilities may end up traveling as three or four distinct parties with support people. Support staff should take good care of themselves (hydration, snacks, sunscreen, etc.) so they can provide undistracted assistance.

Equipment

- People with disabilities may require the following types of equipment: manual and power wheelchairs, crutches, walkers, communication devices, assistive listening equipment, service animals, etc. Instruction may be required to engage or assist with personal equipment.
- Adaptive equipment and supplies, as well as other hiking gear such as daypacks, water bottles, raingear, maps, compasses, etc., should be functional and ready for use prior to the hike.
- Service animals should be included on the hike and allowed to work unobstructed.
- Adaptive equipment needed for hiking includes: all-terrain wheelchairs, baby joggers, crutches, walkers, gait belts.
- A toolkit with extra parts, tire pump, tire patch material, tools, etc. will be necessary to have along for minor adjustments and repairs as needed while on trail.
- Provide helmets as a safety precaution for hikers in chairs and hikers who can walk who have balance problems or brain injuries.

Variations

- Individuals with a disability who can walk participate in a publicly advertised hike.
- A group of individuals with disabilities attends a publicly advertised accessible hiking program.
- An individual with a disability or a group of people with disabilities attends private or custom nature walk.

Addressable Problems

Facilities

Facility access

Facilities used should be fully accessible to provide the best experience. If they are not, the following adaptations may be made. However, the adaptations are not optimum solutions and should not be presented as such.

- Temporary ramps may be installed to provide access up one step into building or restrooms.
- Side entrances may be used to access buildings.
- Additional personal assistance may be required in bathroom, with ADLs (activities of daily living), etc.

Intended route of travel may not be accessible for some participants due to steep grades, gravel, mud, deep sand, water, narrow bridges, etc.

Provide specialized equipment and support services, as required, allowing participants to hike using all-terrain wheelchairs, walkers, crutches, gait belts, and sighted guide support.

Hiking trails are by nature rugged and will present a variety of
obstacles and challenges inherent to the nature of the activity.
There may be roots, rocks, steep grades, muddy sections, stream
crossings, bridges without ramps, bog bridges, fallen trees, etc. These
are best addressed with adequate equipment, plenty of support staff,
and a respect for personal limits. Have enough staff to allow for
traveling and resting at an appropriate pace for each individual. A
positive attitude on the part of the leader and staff is also essential,
recognizing accomplishments, appreciating the environment,
generating good teamwork, etc.

Equipment

Lack of appropriate equipment

People with mobility impairments may require the use of adaptive
equipment that needs to be well maintained and be in good working
order. Equipment should also be appropriate to ruggedness of terrain
in design and appropriate in size for each participant.

Faulty equipment

If any personal equipment is faulty, the owners should be in charge
of any adjustments made to their equipment.

Participants

Prohibitive distance or terrain

Persons with mobility and endurance difficulties should be
accommodated within the group experience whenever possible. If the
nature of the experience would be significantly altered so as to
subtract from the intent of the program, and it is not possible to
reasonably accommodate a particular individual, the original
program should be maintained as is, and a custom program offered to
the individual at another time, if necessary. A ten-mile day hike to
tour a park's remote features might be an example of this.

Lack of information for people with visual impairments
Persons who are visually impaired will be better able to navigate and
enjoy visual aspects of a hike with a sighted guide present who can
provide direction, physical guidance, verbal description, and
assistance in locating tactile opportunities and avoiding dangers.

Communication barrier for people who have hearing impairments
Persons who have a hard time hearing may need assistive listening
equipment, American Sign Language interpretation, or similar
accommodation.

Small print
Any text handouts, maps, etc. should be provided in a large print (14
point) format for people with visual impairments.

Special Considerations

- Mobility impairments
- Diminished endurance
- Vulnerability to temperatures
- Disabilities that affect communications
- Learning disabilities
- Disruptive behavior

Recreation Techniques

General
- Be prepared for outdoor conditions and encourage others to
  arrive prepared.
- Make sure everyone can see and hear instructor prior to starting
  for clear instructions.

- Communicate agenda, route, and make sure everyone is comfortable.
- Allow anyone to drop out during program if needed.
- Choose a route suitable to the abilities and needs of the participants.
- Break participants into smaller hiking groups if they will clearly be hiking at different paces. (Make sure enough staff is present to accommodate this option.)
- Make sure people are noticing, enjoying, and learning something about the environment.
- Provide additional raingear, warm clothes, gloves, hats just in case new hikers come unprepared.
- Take plenty of rest breaks for refueling and rehydration for all hikers.

Adaptive

- Provide all-terrain chairs for wheelchair users to allow greater accessibility over terrain, self-propelling for those who can. Provide one or more people to push as needed.
- Allow people to transfer out of chairs and over rocks or fallen trees as needed.
- Bring portable folding chairs for those who may need to rest frequently, but have difficulty sitting on the ground or uneven surfaces.
- Utilize rickshaw arrangements with front extending poles to allow wheelchair rider to ride in perpetual supported wheelie in steep and rocky situations. One to two people can be positioned at the poles and use hand loops at the pole ends for better handling as needed.
- Have one person assist with pushing chair user from behind, or help brake from behind as needed.

- Approach fallen logs straight on, instead of at an angle, when going over in a chair.

- Utilize tether attachment to chair (held by another hiker) to prevent chair user from going downhill too quickly, or to provide assist with pulling up hills.

- Allow participants with wheelchairs to provide their own seat cushion or utilize foam or other soft material to provide extra cushioning or support as needed.

- Manual wheelchair users should have gloves to protect hands.

- Allow people to walk as much as they can and prefer. Those who are fatigued or in pain may want to use a chair if one is available.

- Some individuals may be able to walk but require balance support. This can be accomplished with a gait belt (a wide belt worn at the waist that can be easily grabbed and held by a support person to assist with balance and physical guidance).

- Shorten route if necessary to accommodate people with endurance issues, e.g., senior citizens.

- Depending on route and participants, it may be advisable to position one or more vehicles along the route (at road crossings) in case someone needs to leave early, or in the event of an accident or injury.

- Provide assistive listening devices as needed. The instructor wears a transmitter. The hiker wears a receiver that can adjust the volume of the instructor's voice. This is great for people who are hard of hearing, people who fall to the rear of the group while traveling, and kids who need a way to focus.

- Minimize the use of scented products, such as bug repellent, during the hike, in case people with chemical sensitivities, allergies, etc. are present.

Risk Management

- Know your hikers and their needs before starting out.
- Know the location.
- Carry a map, sunscreen, water, etc.
- Follow intended route.
- Tell someone when you plan to be back.
- Be prepared for weather. Know the weather forecast.
- For longer excursions: carry water, radio or cell phone, first aid kit, etc.
- For disability groups: make sure enough staff is provided to meet individual needs and monitor individual behavior and communication.
- Observe hiker limits, such as fatigue, loss of attention, and adjust the program accordingly.
- Do not hike in extreme weather conditions.
- Have at risk hikers wear helmets and other safety equipment (such as kneepads), as required.

Program Evaluation

Session reports:
1. Instructors fill out report, one page per session
2. Instructors do a seasonal report including recommendations for future improvements
3. Accessibility survey
4. Record of participant comments during the program
5. Informal post-event interview of participants
6. Analysis of survey and comments

Management evaluation:
1. Assessing incoming information
2. Making adjustments (publicity, equipment, scheduling)

Nature Walks

Marcy Marchello

By choosing accessible locations for nature walks, park visitors using wheelchairs can participate in nature programs.

General Purpose

To include persons of all abilities on nature walks facilitated by one or more environmental educators, in which a group moves through one or more natural environments to experience and learn about various aspects of ecology, natural systems, and the environment.

Outcomes Desired

- Experience of a nature walk as facilitated by an environmental educator in the outdoors
- Opportunities for inclusive socialization and discussion
- Hands-on participation in observational activities
- Opportunities for direct exploration of natural habitats and direct observation of nature

Description of the Program

Facilities

- The route should be fully accessible according to accessibility codes, perhaps an accessible nature trail exists on site, or a good substitute route at least three to five feet wide, with a firm, stable, slip-resistant surface, minimal grades, and no steps onto bridges or platforms. Boardwalks should have wheel-stop edging and boards should run perpendicular to the path of travel and be spaced less than one inch apart.
- Display boards and wayside stations along a trail should be clearly visible by people of any height. Plexiglas coverings should not be milky. If Braille signage is made on metal, be aware that surfaces exposed to the sun may be hot.

Staff

- People leading nature walks should have expertise in the area they are instructing. It as acceptable for their training to have been acquired on site, through interpreter training programs, college degree programs, etc. They should also have some basic disability awareness and etiquette training.
- Staff should be skilled in using adaptive equipment with people with disabilities, have basic first aid and CPR training. Appropriate ratios depend on the participant's requirements and the terrain of the walk. A minimum would be two staff and at least one additional staff for every four participants.

Participants

- Service animals should be allowed to work unobstructed. Respect the needs of the owner and discourage the group from paying too much attention to the animal.

Equipment

- If assistive listening equipment is provided by the environmental educator, it should be charged and operational prior to the walk.
- Any educational tools, props, etc. should be functional and ready for handling and use prior to the walk.

Variations

- Individual with disability participates in publicly advertised nature walk
- Disability group attends publicly advertised nature walk
- Individual with disability or disability group attends private or custom nature walk

Addressable Problems

Facilities

Facility access

Facilities used should be fully accessible to provide the best experience. If they are not, the following adaptations may be made. However, the adaptations are not optimum solutions and should not be presented as such.

- Temporary ramps may be installed to provide access up one step into building or restrooms.
- Side entrances may be used to access buildings.
- Accessible Port-A-Potties may be rented if inside bathrooms are not accessible.
- Additional personal assistance may be required in bathroom, with ADLs (activities of daily living), etc.

Intended route of travel may not be accessible for participants due to steep grades, gravel, mud, deep sand, water, narrow bridges, etc.
Have an alternate route in mind should participants with disabilities be attending.

Educational displays, water fountains, etc. may be too high for use by individuals using wheelchairs.
Ultimately such features should be redesigned. However, temporary measures may be used such as bringing elements of a display down to user level, reading text out loud, passing out a paper map, or filling a cup with water for drinking.

Lack of transportation

If the site is not on a public transportation route, some potential participants may be excluded from the walk.

Equipment

Equipment problems

People with disabilities may have the following types of equipment: manual and power wheelchairs, crutches, communication devices, assistive listening equipment, service animals, etc. Instruction may be required to engage or assist with personal equipment. If any personal equipment is faulty, the owner should be in charge of any adjustments made to his or her equipment.

Participants

Prohibitive distance or terrain

Persons with mobility and endurance difficulties should be accommodated within the group experience whenever possible. If the nature of the experience would be significantly altered so as to subtract from the intent of the program, and it is not possible to reasonably accommodate a particular individual, the original program should be maintained as is, and a custom program offered to the individual at another time, if necessary.

Lack of information for people with visual impairments

Persons who are visually impaired will be better able to navigate and enjoy visual aspects of a nature walk with a sighted guide present who can provide direction, verbal description, and assist in locating tactile opportunities.

Communication barrier for people with hearing impairments

Persons with hearing impairments may need assistive listening equipment, American Sign Language interpretation, or similar accommodation. If videos are used indoors in preparation for a walk, or in lieu of doing a walk on a rainy day, videos should have captioning.

<u>Small print</u>

Any text handouts, maps, etc. should be provided in a large print (14 point) format for people with visual impairments.

Special Considerations

- Mobility impairments
- Diminished endurance
- Vulnerability to temperatures
- Disabilities that affect communications
- Learning disabilities
- Disruptive behavior

Recreation Techniques

General

- Be prepared for outdoor conditions and encourage others to arrive prepared.
- Make sure everyone can see and hear the instructor.
- Communicate agenda, route, and make sure everyone is comfortable.
- Allow anyone to drop out during the program, if needed.
- Speak clearly; use simple language; and avoid complicated, vague, or technical language.
- Provide opportunities that utilize all senses.
- Engage participants in discussion, sensory observation, and comparison.
- Treat everyone equally, solicit feedback from everyone, and use inclusive language and methods.
- Use principles of good nature interpretation.

- Break into smaller groups for observation or other activities if people have different preferences for challenge and learning.

Adaptive

- Educator should speak clearly and make sure everyone can hear him or her and adjust position accordingly. Wait until group is gathered before speaking to everyone as the walk moves from place to place.
- Bring samples of nature to seated individual if subject is out of range (e.g., pond life) and provide presentations at locations where everyone can be present.
- Provide all-terrain or beach chairs for wheelchair users to allow greater accessibility over terrain.
- Choose most accessible route that will allow for educational opportunities.
- Have participants take turns pushing beach chair or being sighted guide to promote inclusive interaction if this suggestion is feasible for the group.
- Allow people to leave their chairs and move to a particular spot if they so desire.
- Shorten route if necessary to accommodate people with endurance issues, e.g., senior citizens.
- Bring portable folding chairs along if feasible.
- Provide assistive listening devices as needed. The instructor wears a transmitter. The hiker wears a receiver that can adjust the volume of the instructor's voice. This is great for people who are hard of hearing, people who fall to the rear of the group while traveling, and kids who need a way to focus.
- Minimize the use of scented products, such as bug repellent, during the walk, in case people with chemical sensitivities, allergies, etc. are present.

Risk Management

- Know your audience, who is attending, the nature of their disabilities, special concerns, etc.
- Know the site.
- Carry a map, sunscreen, water, etc.
- Follow intended route.
- Tell someone when you plan to be back.
- Be prepared for weather. Know the forecast.
- For longer excursions: carry water, radio or cell phone, first aid kit, etc.
- For disability groups: make sure enough staff are available to meet individual needs and monitor individual behavior and communication.
- Observe audience limits, such as loss of attention, and adjust program accordingly.
- Do not go on walks in extreme weather conditions.

Program Evaluation

Session reports:
1. Instructors fill out report, one page per session
2. Instructors do a seasonal report including recommendations for future improvements
3. Accessibility survey
4. Record of participant comments during the program
5. Informal post-event interview of participants
6. Analysis of survey and comments

Management evaluation:
1. Assessing incoming information
2. Making adjustments (publicity, equipment, scheduling)

Flatwater Paddling
(Canoeing and Kayaking)

Marcy Marchello

Paddling through the lily pads gives a different view of nature.

General Purpose

To include persons of all abilities in paddling programs. Participants may have different goals, such as just getting out on the water, playing games, picking blueberries, or learning paddling strokes, and it is recommended to tailor each session according to stated needs as much as possible.

Outcomes Desired

- Learn the basics of paddling in a canoe and kayak
- Opportunity to paddle in a canoe and kayak in a flatwater environment
- Inclusive socialization, hands-on participation, observational learning, helping others
- Opportunities for direct exploration of natural habitats

Description of the Program

Facilities

- Paddling programs can be run from relatively level beaches. It is best if the sand is hard-packed and the beach is not the primary swimming beach.
- The route to the beach should be fully accessible according to accessibility codes. Try to find an accessible walkway to the body of water, or a good route at least three to five feet wide, with a firm, stable, slip-resistant surface, minimal grades, and no steps onto bridges or platforms. Boardwalks should have wheel-stop edging with boards perpendicular to the path of travel and spaced less than one inch apart. Docks should have relatively level gangways and be at least six feet wide for easy

maneuvering.

- Programs operating from such a base can take place all day, serving people on the hour in scheduled time slots. Schedule slots to allow the program to give lessons to the largest number of people.

Staff

- People leading adaptive paddling programs ideally should have professional certification, such as from the American Canoeing Association, which also provides an adaptive paddling endorsement.
- Leaders should be certified in first aid and CPR. Assistive staff may be in school and acquiring training on site.
- If no staff has current lifeguard and waterfront safety certification, a lifeguard should be present, carry a rescue tube, and be able to respond from a boat as well as from the shore if needed. All staff should be experienced paddlers and have basic disability awareness and etiquette training.
- Skilled staff should be out on the water, paddling with participants, and controlling the schedule.
- It is good to have someone on shore while boats go out to answer questions from passersby, register people to paddle, safeguard equipment, catch and stabilize boats as they come back in, etc.
- Standard disability etiquette should be followed by all staff.
- People with cognitive impairments or social difficulties may need one-on-one help to better monitor them and communicate with and for them as needed.

Participants

- If site is accessible, persons with mobility and endurance difficulties are great candidates for paddling as boating can offer a significant amount of freedom, independence, opportunity to rest and let others paddle, as well as the ability to explore otherwise inaccessible natural areas. Temporary solutions may be used to address accessibility issues on shore.

Equipment

- All paddling equipment should be functional and ready prior to the paddling trip. Some adaptations and adaptation materials can already be set up for those known to need them. Conventional canoes and kayaks, paddles, and lifejackets may be used.
- Foam bolster material, duct tape, and bicycle inner tubes should be available to provide adaptations as needed. An empty milk crate with a padded bottom can be useful as an intermediate landing zone for people getting in and out of boats at shore's edge.
- It is good to have a toolkit on hand for equipment set up, take down, and minor repairs as needed.
- A set of boat wheels may be needed for easier transport of boats from storage to the water's edge and back.
- The number of seats in boats will determine how many people can paddle at one time.

Variations

- Individual with disability participates in publicly advertised paddling program.
- Disability group attends publicly advertised paddling program.
- Individual with disability or disability group attends private or custom paddling program.

Addressable Problems

Facilities

Access to beaches and boat ramp

Facilities used should be fully accessible to provide the best experience. If they are not, the following adaptations may be made. However, the adaptations are not optimum solutions and should not be presented as such.

- Temporary ramps may be installed to provide access up one step into buildings or restrooms.
- Mats may be installed outside to provide a solid surface to maneuver wheelchairs or crutches over soft sand.
- Side entrances may be used to access buildings.
- Accessible Port-A-Potties may be rented if inside bathrooms are not accessible.
- Additional personal assistance may be required in bathroom, with ADLs (activities of daily living), etc.

Intended route of travel may not be accessible for all participants due to steep grades, gravel, mud, deep sand, water, narrow bridges, etc.

The best solution is to have an accessible route in mind should participants with disabilities be attending. If this is not possible, additional assistance may be required and some participants may not be able to be accommodated.

Lack of transportation

If the site is not on a public transportation route, some potential participants may be excluded from participating.

Equipment

Equipment issues

People with disabilities may present the following types of equipment: manual and power wheelchairs, crutches, communication devices, assistive listening equipment, service animals, etc. Instruction may be required to engage or assist with personal equipment. If any personal equipment is faulty, the owners should be in charge of any adjustments made to their equipment.

Participants

Cognitive impairments

Persons with cognitive impairments may require any of the following: slower pace, extra time to integrate information, time out to settle down, easy uncomplicated instructions, repetition, focal tasks, etc.

Service animals

Service animals should be allowed to work unobstructed. Respect the needs of the owner and discourage the group from paying too much attention to the animal. Service animals can be left on shore with someone. In some cases they can be included in boats if they can be trusted not to tip the vessel. It is best if the final arrangement is negotiated between the owner and the program leader.

Lack of information for people with visual impairments

Persons who are visually impaired may better navigate terrain and locate boats with a cane, service dog, or sighted guide present.

Communication barrier for people with hearing impairments

Persons with hearing impairments may need assistive listening equipment, American Sign Language interpretation, or similar accommodation. Such arrangements will need to be set up in advance.

Special Considerations

Balance in a canoe or kayak is important. People with erratic behavior, fear of water, weight imbalances (slump to one side), weak upper bodies, inability to sit upright by themselves, etc. will require special consideration and, perhaps, stabilizing equipment such as an outrigger.

Recreation Techniques

General
- Be prepared for outdoor conditions and encourage others to arrive prepared with hat, water, sunscreen, bug repellent, windbreaker, etc.
- Schedule paddlers for one hour time slots through the day, or meet at a designated time for a group paddle.
- Make sure everyone can see and hear the instructor. The instructor should provide introductions, a program overview, and basic instructions with special consideration to newcomers and people who may be anxious.
- The instructor should make any safety precautions very clear to all participants, such as no swimming, no bare feet, everyone wears a lifejacket, etc.
- Instructor should set up paddling partners with attention to everyone's abilities to ensure successful paddling experiences based on participant's goals and needs.
- All boats should be secure on shore while participants are entering and exiting.

Adaptive

- Foam bolsters or padding can be secured around participants, lodged between participant and side of boat, under knees, etc. for additional comfort and stability.

- Personal wheelchair seat cushions can be used on canoe or kayak seats provided the user doesn't mind them getting wet.

- Supportive seating devices can be used for individuals who cannot sit upright and maintain balance on their own.

- Grip aids can be customized with bicycle inner tube sections or Velcro straps and duct tape on canoe and kayak paddles for those with weak grip.

- Pipe foam can be inserted and taped over canoe gunwales or kayak cockpit rims to minimize skin breakdown for people whose legs or arms may be resting against these edges while paddling.

- Conventional canoe seat backs can be used to provide lower back support as needed.

- Alternative kayak paddles may be used to accommodate various abilities and needs. Lightweight paddles allow people with weak endurance or upper body strength to paddle for longer periods of time more comfortably. Paddles with set blades at the same angle eliminate the more complicated maneuver of feathering for less wind resistance.

- Tactile additions to paddles will help people with visual impairments stay oriented to blade direction in the water while paddling. This can be accomplished by taping a small object, such as a bean, to the handle to indicate blade direction.

Risk Management

- Know your participants, the nature of their disabilities, special concerns, etc.
- Make sure sunscreen, water, etc. are available.
- Know the weather forecast.
- If possible, be in radio contact with park staff.
- Have a lifeguard or lifeguard certified staff present.
- All paddlers must wear appropriate lifejacket style and size.
- Use American Canoeing Association requirements for paddlers as a guideline for participation.
- Be comfortable in the water.
- Be able to support head.
- Be able to seal mouth.
- Be able to turn over in water and stay over (independently or through lifejacket design).
- Participants should not be tied down or into any seat in case the canoe tips over.
- For disability groups: make sure enough staff is available to meet individual needs and monitor individual behavior and communication.
- Do not run program in extreme weather conditions. Get off the water if a thunderstorm begins, and do not go out onto the water if thunder and lightning are present.
- All staff should be skilled in canoe and kayak rescue techniques and refresh these skills each season. Rescue practice can and should be incorporated into programs with ongoing participants who are working on their paddling skills. Teaching various rescue methods is also a nice way to cool off on a hot day.

Program Evaluation

Session reports:

1. Instructors fill out report, one page per session
2. Instructors do a seasonal report including recommendations for future improvements
3. Accessibility survey
4. Record of participant comments during the program
5. Informal post-event interview of participants
6. Analysis of survey and comments

Management evaluation:

1. Assessing incoming information
2. Making adjustments (publicity, equipment, scheduling)

Rowing

Marcy Marchello

Rowing program participant transfers himself into an adaptive rowing shell.

General Purpose

To include persons of all abilities in rowing programs. Participants may have different goals, such as just getting out on the water, learning technical skills, working out, or practicing for competition. It is recommended that each session is tailored according to the participants' needs as much as possible.

Outcomes Desired

- Learning the basics of rowing
- Opportunity to row in a flat or slow-moving water environment
- Inclusive socialization, hands-on participation, observational learning, helping others
- Opportunities for exercise, teamwork (physical synchronization of rowing strokes), and possibly competition
- In the event an individual is completely unable to row, the opportunity to get out on the water and enjoy a new perspective

Description of the Program

Facilities

- Rowing programs are best facilitated from accessible docks. Programs operating from accessible docks can take place all day, serving people on the hour in scheduled time slots, to give the most opportunity and basic lessons to the largest number of people.

Staff

- People leading adaptive rowing programs ideally should have previous experience with another adaptive rowing program.

They should be skilled rowers with coaching experience and previous experience working with people with disabilities in a supportive role.

- Leaders should be certified in First Aid and CPR.
- All staff should be experienced rowers and have basic disability awareness and etiquette training.
- Assistive staff may be in school and acquiring training on site.
- A lifeguard should be present, carry a rescue tube, and be able to respond from a boat as well as from the dock, if needed.
- Make sure every boat has a skilled rower who is capable of controlling the boat and watching ahead for obstacles, danger, etc.
- Skilled staff should be out on the water, rowing with participants, and controlling the schedule.
- It is good to have someone on the dock while boats go out, to answer questions of passersby, register people to row, safeguard equipment, monitor the dock environment, catch boats as they come back in, etc.

Participants

- As long as the site is wheelchair accessible, persons with mobility and endurance difficulties are great candidates for rowing, which can offer a significant amount of freedom, independence, and opportunity for exercise.

Equipment

- Wide rowing shells, such as the Alden Ocean Shell, or conventional rowboats can be used. For rowing shells, pontoons are recommended for all beginning rowers for uncompromised stability. Stationary seats, as well as conventional sliding seats may be used, depending on participant's ability to use his or her legs. A variety of oar styles is recommended to accommodate various user needs. Singles, fours, eights, and rowing barges can also be used, based on skill level, individual and group needs, equipment availability, etc.

- All rowing equipment should be functional and ready for handling and use prior to the program.
- The number of seats in boats will determine how many people can row at one time, as well as the number of skilled assistants.
- It is good to have a toolkit on hand for equipment set up, take down, and minor repairs as needed.
- A set of boat wheels may be needed for easier transport of boats from storage to the water's edge and back.

Variations
- An individual with a disability participates in a publicly advertised rowing program.
- A group of individuals with disabilities attends a publicly advertised rowing program.
- An individual with a disability or disability group attends a private or custom rowing program.

Addressable Problems

Facilities
Water safety
Because rowing often takes place on wide river environments, the current and water level are special considerations for safety and physical comfort.

Dock areas may not be accessible for participants using wheelchairs
Facilities used should be fully accessible to provide the best experience. Participants should be able to park near the dock area,

get to an accessible bathroom, and follow an accessible route with zero to moderate grades to the dock. The gangway should be flush to the route surface and at a moderate angle. The dock should be well constructed and at least six feet wide, preferably much wider, to accommodate all users with ease. Water level should be no more than 18" below the top surface of the dock.

Facility access

Facilities used should be fully accessible to provide the best experience. If they are not, the following adaptations may be made. However, the adaptations are not optimum solutions and should not be presented as such.

- Temporary ramps may be installed to provide access up one step into building or restrooms.
- Mats may be installed outside to provide a solid surface to maneuver wheelchairs or crutches over sand.
- Side entrances may be used to access buildings.
- Accessible Port-A-Potties may be rented if inside bathrooms are not accessible.
- Additional personal assistance may be required in bathroom, with ADLs (activities of daily living), etc.

Equipment

Equipment concerns

People with disabilities may present the following types of equipment: manual and power wheelchairs, crutches, communication devices, assistive listening equipment, service animals, etc. Instruction may be required to engage or assist with personal equipment. Some adaptations and adaptation materials can already be set up for users known to need them. If any personal equipment is faulty, the owners should be in charge of any adjustments made to their equipment.

Participants

Service animals

Service animals should be allowed to work unobstructed. Respect the needs of the owner and discourage the group from paying too much attention to the animal. Service animals are best left on the dock with someone.

Cognitive impairments

People with cognitive impairments or social difficulties may need one-on-one help to better monitor them and communicate with and for them as needed. They may also require any of the following: slower pace, extra time to integrate information, time out to settle down, easy uncomplicated instruction, repetition, focal tasks, etc.

Transportation

If the site is not on a public transportation route, some potential participants may be excluded from participating.

Lack of information for people with visual impairments

Persons who are visually impaired will be better able to navigate terrain and locate boats with a cane, service dog, or sighted guide present.

Communication barrier for people with hearing impairments

Persons with hearing impairments may need assistive listening equipment, American Sign Language interpretation, or similar accommodations. Such arrangements will need to be set up in advance.

Special Considerations

- People with erratic behavior, visual impairments, fear of water, weight imbalances (slump to one side), weak or unusable upper bodies, inability to sit upright by themselves, etc. will require special consideration.
- The techniques of rowing are more complicated than paddling, making rowing a more difficult or less desirable activity for some people. This is most likely to come up with people who have difficulty with concentration and coordination.
- With the use of large pontoons, rowing shells are virtually untippable (unless caught in a collision with much larger vessels) and therefore rowing is significantly less risky than paddling in a safe environment.

Recreation Techniques

General

- Be prepared for outdoor conditions and encourage others to arrive prepared with hat, water, sunscreen, bug repellent, windbreaker, etc.
- Schedule rowers for one-hour time slots throughout the day or meet at a designated time for a group rowing experience.
- Make sure everyone can see and hear the instructor. While on the dock, the instructor should provide introductions and basic instructions for what will take place, with special consideration to newcomers and people with any anxiety.
- Instructor should make any safety precautions very clear to all participants, such as no swimming, everyone wears a lifejacket, appropriate dock behavior, etc.
- Instructor can work with beginners in a double for one-on-one instruction and set up intermediate and advanced rowers in

singles, doubles, etc. based on participants' goals and needs.

- All boats should be secured to the dock while participants are entering and exiting.
- Participants must wear some water safety device, usually lifejackets. If participant can inflate a life vest, less cumbersome inflatable designs may be used.
- Groups may prefer a barge experience with participants rowing with one oar each.

Adaptive

- Foam bolsters or padding can be used for additional comfort and stability.
- Personal wheelchair seat cushions can be used on rowing seats provided the user doesn't mind them getting wet.
- Stationary seats can be used by people who don't use their legs to row. If these seats have a high back, individuals with weak torso strength or poor upper body balance can be strapped in at chest level for secure seating. Strapping people into boats is only recommended if large pontoons are used and tipping the boat is virtually impossible.
- Grip aids can be created using an ace bandage applied over hands and oar handles. This is usually quite effective for people with weak grip, but should only be done on boats with large pontoons.
- Alternate oar styles may be used based on participant ability and need. Different blade styles with less surface area may allow weaker participants to row farther with more enjoyment and less muscle strain. Oar designs that don't turn in the oarlock (which eliminates feathering techniques) may make the rowing motion easier for people who are overwhelmed by having to think about so many things at once.

- Tactile additions to oars will help people with visual impairments stay oriented to blade direction in the water while rowing. This can be accomplished by taping a small object, such as a bean, to the oar handle to indicate blade direction.

Risk Management

- Know your participants, the nature of their disabilities, special concerns, etc.
- Make sure sunscreen, water, etc. is available.
- Know the weather forecast.
- If possible, be in radio contact with park staff.
- Have a lifeguard or lifeguard certified staff present.
- Have all rowers wear appropriate lifejacket style and size.
- For disability groups: make sure staff is available to meet individual needs and monitor individual behavior and communication.
- Do not row in extreme weather conditions. Get off the water if a thunderstorm begins, and do not go out onto the water if thunder and lightning are present.

Program Evaluation

Session reports:
1. Instructors fill out report, one page per session
2. Instructors do a seasonal report including recommendations for future improvements
3. Accessibility survey
4. Record of participant comments during the program
5. Informal post-event interview of participants
6. Analysis of survey and comments

Management evaluation:
1. Assessing incoming information
2. Making adjustments (publicity, equipment, scheduling)

All Seasons

- **Nature Photography**

Introduction to Nature Photography

Cyndy Chamberland

Pausing on the trail to take a close-up of flowers.

General Purpose

To introduce persons of all abilities to the basics of nature photography.

Outcomes Desired

- Knowledge and skills to take photographs outdoors as independently as possible
- Opportunity for inclusive socialization
- Understanding of basic low-cost equipment that is needed to pursue photography as an outdoor activity

Description of the Program

Facilities

- The nature photography program is designed to introduce participants to the basics of photography. Participants will have an opportunity to take pictures in state parks or other natural areas with accessible trails and scenic areas where pictures may be taken. Private gardens and wildlife areas may also be used, as long as the fees are within the budgets of the participants. All facilities should have accessible parking and restrooms.

Staff

- There should be a minimum of two staff available that are proficient in first aid, CPR, and disability and awareness training. Have an additional staff or volunteer for every four participants. If participants are going out separately, the staffing ratio will need to be higher, one or more people to assist each participant.
- Staff and volunteers should be competent in basic photography.

- Have enough staff to accommodate the number of people and types of disabilities (pre-registration).
- A sign language interpreter should be brought in for anyone who is hearing impaired and communicates through sign language.

Equipment

- Equipment will be low cost and store bought.
- Digital cameras are becoming inexpensive enough that the program or participant may consider using one of them instead of film.
- Participants may bring their own camera of any type or purchase a disposable 35-millimeter camera for use at each class. Participants should use 400-speed film.
- Participants will need to assume cost for film developing and printing.

Variations

- Individual with disability participates in publicly advertised nature photography program.
- Disability group attends publicly advertised nature photography program.
- Individual with disability or disability group attends private or custom nature photography program.

Addressable Problems

Facilities

Facility access

Facilities used should be fully accessible to provide the best experience. If they are not, the following adaptations may be made. However, the adaptations are not optimum solutions and should not be presented as such.

- Temporary ramps may be installed to provide access up one step into building or restrooms.
- Side entrances may be used to access buildings.
- Accessible Port-A-Potties may be rented if inside bathrooms are not accessible.
- Additional personal assistance may be required in bathroom, with ADLs (activities of daily living), etc.

Park facilities may not be accessible for participants using wheelchairs

Trails may be too steep, soft, muddy, or rocky inhibiting wheelchair mobility. Accessible trails, fields, etc. should be used for participants who require them.

Equipment

Program may not be accessible for persons with severe visual disabilities.

Participants with severe visual disabilities will likely require additional adaptive equipment such as a camera with magnifying lenses. Digital cameras with a preview screen may be easier for some participants to use.

Participants

Cognitive disabilities

Participants with cognitive disabilities may require extra assistance in taking pictures.

Special Considerations

Participants with behavioral problems may require special consideration.

Recreation Techniques

General

- Be prepared for outdoor conditions. Insure that participants arrive prepared.
- At beginning of each session have participants meet indoors or at a sheltered location in the park (if possible) for basic instruction.
- Instructor will give a group introduction to photography. Lessons will include basic camera operation, light, composition, focusing, special effects, film speed, color and black and white, and master nature photographers.
- After each lesson, participants will be assigned different tasks to complete in the field. Here participants will team up or individually go off in the park and take photographs for assigned tasks.
- Staff and volunteers will assist participants with completing tasks outdoors.
- Staff and volunteers will assist participants as needed during the program but promote participant's independence as much as possible.
- Staff and volunteers will use motivational techniques such as praising participants for composition, lighting, pictures, etc.
- At the end of each lesson, the group will reconvene to summarize their experiences for that assignment.
- At the beginning of each subsequent lesson, participants will share their developed pictures from the previous session and critique their work.

Adaptive

- Choose an accessible site.
- Assist participants with camera use as needed. Disposable cameras are essentially problem free and simple to operate even

with limited dexterity.
- Staff and volunteers can provide one-on-one assistance to participants with mobility, visual or hearing impairments, or developmental disabilities as needed.

Risk Management

- Participants should be encouraged to stay near the group meeting place for safety measures.
- Make sure participants are dressed appropriately, including shoes or sneakers (no bare feet).
- Provide a protected area for instruction and to get out of the rain or sun.
- Have staff, volunteers, and participants sign waiver forms prior to starting the course.
- Know and follow the emergency management and incident report protocols of the facility.
- Know and have ready access to the person on duty at the facility.
- Be aware of what's going on in the program including levels of risk.
- Staff should be covered by insurance.
- Program should run in good weather conditions. Have a safe place that you can get to quickly in case of thunderstorms.
- Participants should bring cold water for hydration if weather is warm or sunny.

Program Evaluation

Session reports:
1. Instructors fill out report, one page per session

2. Instructors do a seasonal report including recommendations for future improvements
3. Accessibility survey
4. Record of participant comments during the program
5. Informal post-event interview of participants
6. Analysis of survey and comments

Management evaluation:
1. Assessing incoming information
2. Making adjustments (publicity, equipment, scheduling)

Chapter Four

Developing the Individual's Program

Donald R. Snyder
Anne M. Rothschadl
Angela M. Cullinan

Introduction

The purpose of this chapter is to provide a systematic individual recreation plan that can be modified for schools and the community. This individual recreation plan is based on the original Peterson and Gunn model for specific program design, which is adaptable to clinical and non-clinical (community, school, and agency) settings. The authors refer to this diagram as the STEP to C then P Individual Program Plan Diagram, as shown below.

STEP to C then P Individual Program Plan Diagram

S.......... Statement of Purpose

T......... Terminal Performance Objective

E......... Enabling Outcomes

P .... Performance Measures

to

C......... Content and Process Descriptions

then

P .... Performance Sheets

The following pages show an example of using the STEP to C then P process to describe a cycling program. For a full program, there would be a C page (Content and Process Description) for each enabling outcome.

S

Statement of Purpose

To provide a cycling program that promotes and improves cardiovascular fitness, strength, endurance, and socialization opportunities, including the psychosocial benefits of increased self-esteem, efficacy, and resiliency.

T

Terminal Performance Objective

To ride a cycle outdoors using adapted equipment with increased knowledge of the activity and increased level of independence in cycling compared to knowledge and level of independence before participation in program.

E

Enabling Outcomes

1. Knowledge of bicycling techniques
2. Knowledge of rules and traffic regulations
3. Ability to read maps
4. Pedaling techniques for speed and endurance
5. Knowledge of equipment
6. Knowledge of basic repair techniques
7. Basic familiarity with trails and roads
8. Understanding of bicycle etiquette
9. Knowledge of appropriate hydration and nutrition

P

Performance Measure

Under the supervision of an Outdoor/Therapeutic Recreation Specialist, the client will select an appropriate bicycle; use the correct cycling form, as indicated in the cycling protocol; demonstrate the ability to make simple repairs; and participate in a half-hour ride following traffic laws and bicycling etiquette.

C

Content and Process Description

Terminal Performance Objective *ride a cycle outdoors*

Enabling Outcome *5. Knowledge of equipment*

Content	Process
1. selecting equipment	1. Instruction and demonstration of selecting equipment of the right size and adapted modifications to allow a safe and pleasant ride.
2. wheels and tires	2. Instruction and demonstration of changing tires and patching a blowout.
3. gears	3. Demonstration of shifting techniques and which gears are appropriate.
4. cycle security	4. Discussion of how to prevent the cycle from being stolen and instruction on how to lock cycle.
5. frame, brakes, other safety concerns	5. Learn simple points to check to make sure the cycle is safe to ride.

P

Performance Sheet

Program: Cycling

Enabling outcome (W= worked on, C= completed)									
Sessions 1	2	3	4	5	6	7	8	9	...
1									
2									
3									
4									
5									
...									

Chapter Five

Common Disabling Conditions

Anne M. Rothschadl with students
Marcy Marchello
Will Blaschko

Introduction to Serving People with Disabilities

At least 20% of the overall population, or some 54 million people residing in the U.S. today, are considered to have disabilities. People with disabilities are represented in every cross-section of society: age, race, class, education, gender, and religion. Disabilities may be obvious or hidden. They may be temporary or permanent. People may have one disability or several. Their condition may be constant or may come and go, depending on a variety of circumstances. Disabilities may affect physical function, cognitive ability, sensory experience, and emotional behavior. They may have originated in the person's genetic material, in the womb, at birth, or have been acquired later in life through accident, illness, or aging. Passage of the Americans with Disabilities Act of 1990 established the right of all Americans to access public settings and programs, and was a major reason why the Department of Conservation and Recreation, as well as many other government agencies across the country, addressed issues of accessibility.

This chapter contains a listing of various disabilities, impairments, and conditions, using common terms and definitions. This reference is supplied with the intention to provide easy-to-understand information for anyone who might be working with people with disabilities as part of the general public or in specialized programs. In some cases staff may have had prior medical training and know what it means to be "T-6 para" or have "Asperger's" or "tachycardia." Often students, volunteers, outdoor recreation leaders, and others who find themselves canoeing or skiing with participants who are disabled do not have the formal training in this area that lends an immediate understanding of terminology. Sometimes people with disabilities are happy to explain their disability, often they'd prefer not to be a spokesperson for their disability. Ready access to a reference list can help staff grasp the essentials of a diagnosis without "prying" and let the staff ask relevant questions of participants to assist them in their recreation experience.

Gathering advance information about participants is certainly relevant. For instance, persons with traumatic brain injury (TBI) can present a variety of symptoms across the physical, cognitive, and emotional spectrum. Some may use wheelchairs and others may be able to walk. Some may have communication difficulty. Some may display a lack of inhibition. Others may not exhibit any unusual characteristics or behavior. The more the staff knows in advance, the better prepared they will be to take the steps necessary to create the most successful recreation experience possible.

While knowing terms or diagnoses is helpful, in the field it is not so much the terminology as zeroing in on what people can and can't do that is essential. It needs to be done in a way that does not negate people for not being able to do some things. The question should not be, "Can you paddle?" It should be "Can you grip this paddle this way?" or "Can you use your abdominal muscles?" or "Can you push this arm forward while pulling this arm back?" to break down the activity into understandable components of ability. The places where a "can't" presents itself are likely to be the places where an adaptation is required. Position, movement, and tasks can be greatly assisted through the creative use of many common items, such as duct tape, ensolite foam, and Velcro straps. Homemade or professionally manufactured assistive devices are also desirable in order to easily accommodate the range of people who may show up at programs. Having ready solutions in mind is one of the benefits gained by knowing the participants. Often people with disabilities are willing to be patient about solutions and assist the adaptation process with their own wealth of experience and assistive devices.

While creativity is a critical component in serving such a diverse population and meeting individuals with a wide variety of unique characteristics in recreational settings, careful attention to respect is also vital. The DCR Universal Access Program has trained many park staff, volunteers, and outdoor leaders over the years in the basic essentials of disability awareness and etiquette. When the people in the parks who will be greeting or instructing people with disabilities are savvy to appropriate communication methods, park visitors with disabilities recognize they are welcome. Without proper awareness and etiquette, it can be all too easy to inadvertently insult someone. The following is a quick reference of points of etiquette that the DCR uses to best respond to visitors with disabilities:

1. Remember people are people first. A disability is just one of many characteristics someone might have.
2. Speak directly to the individual with the disability, even if people are present with whom it might be easier to communicate.
3. Address people by their name.
4. Speak in a normal tone of voice, with normal volume, and normal mouth movements, unless asked to do otherwise.
5. Avoid the use of the word "handicapped," as well as other words that may be considered offensive, such as "gimp," "retarded," etc.
6. Ask how you can best help someone and follow his or her guidance. Accept "yes" as yes, and "no" as no.
7. Be friendly, respectful, take your time, relax, and allow things to take longer.
8. Assume normal intelligence in people you meet. Speak to and treat individuals as you would prefer to be spoken to and treated. People with severe disabilities can often hear normally.
9. Respect personal space — do not touch anyone unless appropriate. Ask before touching or moving wheelchairs, crutches, etc. These items are considered part of personal space.
10. Respect independence, even if it appears to you that someone needs help.
11. Avoid making assumptions about what people can and can't do.
12. Service animals are allowed.
13. Do not pretend you understand if you do not when speaking with someone with a speech difficulty. Be patient, give your full attention, use resources (pen and paper, keyboard, etc.), and keep trying until you understand. Keep your manner encouraging. Ask questions that require short answers or a nod or shake of the head when necessary. Repeat what you do understand and build from there.

14. When having a conversation of more than a few minutes with someone using a wheelchair, shift to their eye level by kneeling, sitting on a chair, etc.

15. It's okay to use phrases like "see you later" to someone who is visually impaired, or "let's go for a walk" to someone using a wheelchair.

16. Wave your hand, or tap a person's shoulder when trying to get the attention of someone who has a hearing loss.

17. Use simple, concise language for people with cognitive impairments. Showing instead of telling is helpful.

18. Consider distance, weather, surfaces, and inclines when providing directions for wheelchair users.

19. Introduce yourself by name to people who are visually impaired and use their name when speaking directly to them. Let them know when you are ending a conversation or moving away from them.

20. Allow people with visual impairments to take you by the arm if they wish in order to be guided. Let them know of any steps or changes in level. Use specifics such as left or right. Offer seating by placing their hand on the back or arm of a seat.

Further elaboration of disability etiquette is often available from agencies or organizations that serve specific populations. The above principles are standard and, when put into practice, will go far towards creating a welcoming environment for people with disabilities. Positive, informed attitudes, combined with accessible sites, adaptive equipment, adaptation supplies, solid safety management planning and policies, and skilled and qualified program staff practically ensure that program participants with disabilities will be well served in recreation programs.

One last significant factor is, of course, getting the word out to potential participants with disabilities. Including accessibility information, such as the phrase "wheelchairs available" or "assistive listening equipment available" on program calendars or flyers is a vital first step. Just letting the public know which programs are basically accessible — or if they truly are not — is all too often overlooked in most regular media advertising. Beyond this essential practice, information on brochures can be made available on audio tape for people who are visually impaired, brochures and maps can be copied in a larger print size for people with visual impairments, press releases can be sent to local organizations that serve people with disabilities, and so forth. Press releases should include a contact number for people who may need reasonable accommodations for accessibility. If information is provided to the public through the internet, standard guidelines should be followed to ensure that all users are able to access the website including web creation standards for clients with visual impairments. By informing the public in appropriate formats with essential information about accessibility, a truly welcoming and inclusive stance will be established, and this is a vital foundation for any adaptive or inclusive program.

Cardiovascular Disabilities

Persons with cardiovascular disabilities may suffer from one or more of the following:

- aneurysm: the dilation or bulging out of the wall of an artery or vein. It may rupture and cause a spontaneous hemorrhage (burlingame, 2001).

- cardiac arrhythmias: failure in the sinus node's pace-making function or the electrical conduction system that causes an irregular cardiac rate and/or rhythm.

- coronary artery disease (atherosclerosis): a disorder in which too much cholesterol builds up in the blood and accumulates on the walls of the blood vessels, generally affecting the large vessels coming from the heart. One of a varied number of conditions that cause various pathologic effects. The most common disease is coronary atherosclerosis, the leading cause of death in the Western world (burlingame, 2001).

- endocarditis: inflammation of the inner lining of the heart; when untreated, it can be fatal.

- heart failure: inability of the heart to pump enough blood for the body's metabolic functions to continue.

- primary/essential hypertension: persistently elevated arterial blood pressure (burlingame, 2001).

- valvular heart disease: disorder of a cardiac valve. One of its characteristics is obstructed blood flow or regurgitation of blood. Valves become stiff and calcified or otherwise damaged.

Respiratory Disorders

- asthma: chronic disorder that produces episodic, reversible airway obstruction. This obstruction may be caused by bronchial spasms, an increase in mucous secretion, and/or an increase in mucosal edema. It is most often caused by allergic reactions to an environmental irritant, a specific type of food, or stress. Approximately 10 million Americans (3-4% of the population) have asthma. Asthma symptoms include severe wheezing, difficulty breathing, and a sensation of tightness in the chest. Cyanosis, confusion, and lethargy signal a life-threatening situation (burlingame, 2001). Factors that can exacerbate asthma include rapid changes in temperature or humidity, allergies, upper respiratory infections, exercise, stress, and smoke.

- cystic fibrosis (CF): disorder of the exocrine system that causes a thickening of saliva, mucus, and sweat. This inherited disorder has two primary impacts on the patient's functional ability: 1. recurrent infections of the lungs due to thickened mucus that lines the lungs, trapping bacteria and 2. small stature due, in part, to abnormal mucus secretions that interfere with the flow of digestive enzymes (incomplete digestion). Cause: CF is a recessive genetic trait and requires that both parents be carriers of the CF recessive gene. Impact on functional ability: The chronic lung infections and the abnormal digestive action cause the youth with CF to have less energy than most of his/her peers and to miss a fair amount of school and other activities due to time spent in the hospital. The older the youth gets, the more frequent the hospitalizations become. Few individuals with CF live past their 20s (burlingame, 2001).

- emphysema: chronic disease that affects the ability of the patient's lungs to exchange gases. Generally, the elasticity of the lung walls has been destroyed resulting in a chronic shortness of breath, dyspnea, and coughing along with potential restlessness and confusion secondary to a lack of oxygen.

- occupational lung diseases: occupational hazard associated with the repeated inhalation of dust, silica, asbestos, and other fine materials that leads to fibrosis, scarring, and abnormal conditions of the lungs.

- tuberculosis (TB): chronic infection caused by the TB bacteria — Mycobacterium tuberculosis. While TB is a chronic lung infection, individuals with AIDS may experience a spread of the infection to multiple organs. Fatigue, chest pain, weight loss, and fever are early signs of TB. TB requires long-term antibiotic treatment (burlingame, 2001). TB is transmitted from person to person by an aerosol of organisms suspended in tiny droplets that are inhaled.

Endocrine Disorders

- Addison's disease: endocrine disorder that generally occurs when 90% or more of the adrenal gland is destroyed. The most common cause of this destruction is an autoimmune system failure. Some of the primary symptoms of Addison's disease are a bronze coloration of the skin and gastrointestinal disorders (including nausea, vomiting, anorexia, and chronic diarrhea). The patient will likely also complain about weakness and fatigue. Weight loss is common (burlingame, 2001).

- Cushing's syndrome: disorder resulting from the excessive production of cortisol in the adrenal cortex. Patients may have decreased glucose tolerance, obesity, and moon faces. The disorder also can lower levels of testosterone and make menstrual periods scant.

- diabetes insipidus: disorder caused by damage to the neurohypophyseal system that results in a large excretion of urine and an excessive thirst. This is caused by deficient production of the antidiuretic hormone or by the kidney tubules' inability to respond to ADH.

- diabetes mellitus: disorder in the body's production and use of insulin and in the body's use of blood sugar resulting in a high blood glucose level. Diabetes has both short-term and long-term consequences. Individuals with diabetes have a disorder that causes the abnormal metabolism of carbohydrates, fats, and proteins (burlingame, 2001).

- hyperthyroidism: condition of increased secretions from the thyroid gland usually followed by accelerated metabolic processes, nervousness, tremor, constant hunger, weight loss, fatigue, and heat intolerance.

- hypothyroidism: disorder in which the thyroid activity is deficient causing a reduced basal metabolic rate, lethargy, and sensitivity to cold. In women (it affects a higher percentage of women), hypothyroidism may also lead to menstrual disturbances (burlingame, 2001).

Musculoskeletal and Connective Tissue Disabilities

- amputation: removal of a part of the body including cutting through the bone (burlingame, 2001). Levels of upper extremity amputation are
  - o forequarter or interscapular-thoracic amputation: a procedure that removes the entire arm, the scapula, and part of the upper midsection.
  - o shoulder disarticulation (S/D): amputation of the arm at the shoulder joint.
  - o above the elbow (A/E): amputation of the arm between the shoulder and elbow joint.
  - o elbow disarticulation (E/D): amputation of the arm at the elbow joint.
  - o Below elbow (B/E): amputation of the arm anywhere between the elbow and the wrist.
  - o Wrist disarticulation (W/D); amputation of the hand at the wrist.
  - o Partial hand: amputation of one or more fingers or the loss of a portion of the hand.

  Levels of lower extremity amputation:
  - o Hemipelvectomy or hindquarter amputation: amputation of half the pelvis and the entire lower limb. The most severe lower extremity amputation.
  - o Hip disarticulation (H/D): amputation of the leg at the hip joint.
  - o Above the knee (A/K): amputation of the leg above the knee joint but below the hip joint.
  - o Knee disarticulation (K/D): amputation of the lower leg at the knee.

o   Below the knee (B/K): amputation located between the knee and the ankle.

o   Syme's amputation: the amputation of the foot through the ankle joint.

o   Transmetatarsal or partial foot: amputation of a portion of the foot.

- ankylosing spondylitis: systematic inflammatory disease of unknown origin that affects the spine and then adjacent structures. It reduces flexibility in the spine and can include stiffness in other joints and difficulty expanding the rib cage to breathe.

- carpal tunnel syndrome: painful compression of the median nerve in the carpal tunnel in the wrist. Functionally, the individual will experience weakness, pain, tingling, burning, and aching with potential atrophy. Individuals usually also experience a sensory loss in the first three fingers, limiting their ability to function normally in activities of daily living (burlingame, 2001).

- osteoarthritis: type of arthritis that leads to degenerative changes and deformities in the joints. Osteoarthritis has numerous causes that impact the patient's condition. Some of the conditions that may be factors in the development and progression of osteoarthritis include disease processes, trauma, genetic disorders, and obesity (burlingame, 2001).

- osteoporosis: reduction in the mineral content and internal structure of bone mass that may cause a reduction in stature. Osteoporosis is caused by the aging process (postmenopausal women, the primary cause) or by immobility (casting, paralysis, etc., the secondary cause). Patients with osteoporosis have an increased risk for bone fractures and can experience chronic pain (burlingame, 2001).

- rheumatoid arthritis: potentially disabling disability that causes inflammation of a joint or joints. The symptoms of arthritis that may interfere with a patient's level of activity include pain, swelling, stiffness, and weakness (burlingame, 2001).

- systemic lupus erythematosus: an inflammatory disease of connective tissue occurring predominantly in women (90%). It is usually considered to be an autoimmune disease although some people suggest the involvement of a mycobacterium (burlingame, 2001).

- tendonitis: inflammation of a tendon, sometimes, but not always, the result of a sprain.

Traumatic Brain Injury

Injury to the brain as a result of a traumatic event. There are two major classes of brain injuries: open head and closed head.

An *open head injury* is one that penetrates the scalp or skull such as a gun shot wound.

A *closed head injury* results in brain damage without penetration of the scalp or skull and may be due to an impact (e.g., being hit on the head by a baseball) or acceleration/deceleration (e.g., being hit from behind in your car while wearing your seatbelt). The skull may or may not be fractured in a closed head injury (burlingame, 2001).

Inside the Brain

Brain damage is categorized into two distinct types: focal and diffuse. Diffuse damage occurs when a large portion of the brain is damaged due to a collision between the skull and the brain during a closed head injury — often leading to tearing of brain tissues. In the brain, the frontal and temporal lobes, as well as the brain stem, are more likely to be injured due to their proximity to bony protrusions in the skull. Damage to particular areas of the brain can lead to the following symptoms:

- Brain stem: frustration, disorientation, and anger.
- Temporal lobes: behavior disorders, seizures, and communication difficulties.
- Frontal lobes: impulsiveness and lack of judgment.

Damage to the brain is classified in three different ways: tearing, bruising (also called bleeding), and swelling.

- Bruising: When a brain is injured, blood vessels can tear. The blood then collects inside the brain cavity and presses against the sensitive tissues. The tissues affected by the pressure die, possibly causing severe loss in critical parts of the brain.

- Tearing: Brain injuries can cause microscopic tears in the brain that are impossible to find even with CT scans or MRIs. The damaged connections of the neurons lead to a corresponding loss of cognitive function.
- Swelling: When the body realizes that the brain has been injured, extra help is sent to assist in the healing of the damaged area. This extra help can put pressure on other parts of the brain, and those affected parts can die off, causing severe loss in critical parts of the brain (www.tbifyi.com).

Neurological Disorders

- amyotrophic lateral sclerosis (ALS): also known as Lou Gehrig disease. ALS is a degenerative disease of the lower motor neurons and pyramidal tracts. This degeneration causes the individual to experience progressive motor weakness and spastic conditions of his/her limbs. The disease progresses through muscular atrophy, fibrillary twitching, and eventual involvement of the nuclei in the medulla. Death results within two to five years (burlingame, 2001).

- cerebral palsy (CP): chronic neurological disorder developed prenatally, at birth, or shortly thereafter. A patient with CP has anatomically normal muscles and nerves. The disability is caused by the brain's inability to control the muscles and nerves. The two primary functions impacted by CP are movement and communication. The range of functional impairment varies from patient to patient and depends on the location of the damage to the brain (burlingame, 2001).

- epilepsy: disorders of the central nervous system (CNS) that are manifested by seizure activity that must meet all three of the following criteria: 1. the seizure activity is of rapid onset, 2. the actual duration of the seizure activity is short in duration and 3. the reoccurrence of the seizure activity is chronic (burlingame, 2001). Types of epilepsy include:

  o *grand mal epilepsy* (major epilepsy, haut mal epilepsy): The grand mal seizure is large and may include: 1. tonic seizure: loss of consciousness, stiffening of body, irregular breathing, drooling, possible incontinence or 2. clonic seizure: jerking

caused by alternating rigidity and relaxation of muscles for as
little as 10 seconds or as long as 30 minutes (burlingame, 2001).

o *petit mal epilepsy*: petit mal epilepsy is hard to recognize and
   may include loss of consciousness without loss of muscle tone
   (spacing out) and rapid blinking. These last between 5 and 20
   seconds and happen more than 20 times a day (burlingame,
   2001).

o *psychomotor epilepsy* (temporal lobe): This type of epilepsy is
   more common in adults and consists of involuntary repetitive
   actions including rubbing of hands and lip smacking. Lasting
   between 10 and 60 seconds, these rarely occur more than once
   daily. One may also experience changes of emotion after such a
   seizure (burlingame, 2001).

o *autonomic epilepsy* (diencephalic): epilepsy that propagates
   through the centers that control autonomic functions. Symptoms
   can include flushing, pallor, tachycardia, hypertension,
   perspiration, or other processes controlled by the autonomic
   system. Many epileptic seizures show some symptoms of
   involvement of the autonomic system.

• Huntington's disease: hereditary disease characterized by the
  progressive deterioration of the patient's cognitive ability and also an
  erratic deterioration of the patient's involuntary muscle movements.
  There is no cure for the disease at this point although there is a test to
  determine if an individual is carrying the gene for the disease.

• multiple sclerosis (MS): chronic disabling disease of the central
  nervous system. There are two forms of MS: the relapsing/remitting
  type and the chronic type that progressively gets worse. Most new
  cases are adults between the ages of 20 and 40, more often women
  than men. During the course of the disease scattered areas of the

myelin covering of the nerves degenerate. The destruction of this myelin covering causes a "short-circuiting" or blocking of the impulses that control a person's actions. The areas that have the degenerated patches are called plaques. As these areas of plaques combine to make larger holes in the myelin covering, the nerve impulses are not able to function correctly and the message that the nerve was carrying is lost in part or in whole. If the nerve carries information needed for muscle movement, the movement will be weak or absent. If the nerve carries information involving sensation, numbness or tingling may be felt (burlingame, 2001).

- paralysis: complete loss of voluntary movement or motor function in a part due to damage of the neural or muscular mechanism. Paralysis can be distinguished as traumatic, syphilitic, toxic, etc., according to its cause or as obturator, ulnar, etc., according to the nerve part or the muscle affected.

- paraplegia: paralysis of the lower half of the body, often caused by spinal cord damage.

- Parkinson's disease: chronic disease that results from neurological damage to the substantia nigra in the basal ganglia. Usually developing later in life, Parkinson's disease is most commonly known by the muscular tremors, peculiar gait, and stereotypic facial expression. Those with the disease progressively lose sensory-motor coordination and have difficulty initiating activity. Activity requires excessive energy causing individuals to tire quickly (burlingame, 2001).

- post-polio syndrome: set of conditions that appear after recovery from polio, sometimes years later. Some effects of post-polio syndrome include fatigue, weakness, joint and muscle pain, breathing difficulty, and intolerance of cold. There is also the possibility of increased muscle damage and pain. The severity of problems may range from a modest worsening to muscular atrophy. One affected by post-polio syndrome might find it difficult to lift, bend, or stand for a prolonged period of time, walk, climb stairs, push a wheelchair, sleep, swallow, dress, or any other activities requiring muscle strength.

- spinal cord injuries: injury to the nerves in the spine. After a spinal cord injury the loss of function is determined by the level of the spinal cord where the injury occurred, the severity of the injury, and the anatomical portion of the cord body involved. The "level" of the spinal cord injury is determined by the nerve(s) injured (not the vertebra involved). These nerves are classified according to the level of the cord at which they emerge (e.g., C-5 refers to an injury of the spinal cord at the fifth nerve of the cervical segment). The results of the damage depend on the location of the injury.

- stroke: a condition stemming from a lack of oxygen to the brain that could lead to either temporary or permanent paralysis and other loss of function. When the brain cells do not receive the oxygen contained in the blood, they start to die. The restricted blood flow may be due to an occlusion (blockage) by an embolus or by a thrombus (clogging of the artery), or from a cerebrovascular hemorrhage. The effects depend on two factors: 1. the location in the brain that is affected and 2. the intensity of the interruption (how much blood was cut off from the cells). The severity of the symptoms may decrease the first few days after a stroke because reduced swelling of the brain allows normal blood flow to resume in the undamaged parts of the brain (burlingame, 2001).

- tetraplegia: paralysis of all four limbs (arms and legs) due to a high spinal cord injury or stroke.

Dermatologic Disabilities

- allergic contact dermatitis: the body's response after being exposed to an allergen to which the person is hypersensitive. The majority of these are dyes and perfumes, but metals, poison ivy, and chemicals have also been known to cause this reaction.

- basal cell carcinoma: also called basal cell epithelioma, basaloma, carcinoma basocellulare, hair matrix carcinoma. A malignant epithelial cell tumor that begins as a papule, expanding peripherally. Basal cell carcinoma can appear as an oozing, bleeding, unhealing sore or a small reddish growth. The primary cause of this type of cancer is overexposure to radiation or sunlight.

- hives: the non-medical term for urticaria. They are caused by drugs, foods, insect bites, inhalants, stress, exposure to either heat or cold, and exercise. Welts form on the skin, itching and lasting a few hours before completely fading away. New hives appear as old ones disappear. The actual size of the hives varies from pea-sized to much larger. The normal treatment includes antihistamines and the removal of the allergen or stimulus.

- Lyme disease: a tick-borne, inflammatory disease that initially causes fever, stiffness, and rash. The distinguishing early symptom is the "bull's eye" rash at the site of the tick bite. Arthritis-like symptoms and cardiac problems appear in later stages. There is a limited chance that dogs (or other animals allowed outside) that are used in pet therapy programs could carry the ticks. All animals used in pet therapy programs should be examined prior to interacting with patients.

- nickel allergy: also called nickel dermatitis; a contact dermatitis caused by exposure to nickel. Nickel intolerance is usually developed through the use of nickel-containing jewelry. The symptoms include an allergic skin rash that worsens with sweat. Nickel is a common element in watches, jewelry, but can also be found in the workplace or near industries that use nickel. Women seem to be more susceptible than men to this allergy because of their higher rate of body piercing.

- psoriasis: chronic skin disorder that varies in severity from person to person and is subject to "flare-ups." Psoriasis is caused by the over-production of epithelial cells. Psoriasis patches are reddish on the outside with white, dry scales making up the center of the patch (burlingame, 2001).

- vitiligo: condition of the skin of unknown cause. It is benign and creates patches of skin that are devoid of pigment by attacking the pigmentation producing cells. Exposed areas of skin are the most commonly affected. Extreme care must be taken during exposure to sunlight.

Psychiatric Disabilities

- anxiety disorders: Anxiety is the psychological and physical response to an exaggerated, imagined danger or imagined pending discomfort. In response to this imagined or over-emphasized threat, the patient may experience an increased heart rate, change in breathing rate, sweating, fatigue, weakness, choking, nausea or abdominal distress, numbness, dizziness or unsteadiness, hot flashes or chills, and/or trembling. While anxiety is seldom so severe that it makes a normally functional patient non-functional, it can interfere with the patient's ability to integrate into his/her community (burlingame, 2001).

- bipolar disorder: major affective disorder in which there are episodes of both mania and depression; formerly called manic-depressive psychosis, circular, or mixed type. Bipolar disorder may be subdivided into manic, depressed, or mixed types on the basis of currently presenting symptoms. Bipolar I disorder refers to mood swings that are manic in nature. Bipolar II disorder refers to mood swings that are hypomanic (less severe than mania) in nature (burlingame, 2001).

- depression: feeling of sadness or grief. In patients with cerebrovascular accidents (CVA), this depression can be psychological and/or physiological. Depression is a mood state with many different possible diagnoses; some describing the severity and some describing a cause. The symptoms must also be significant enough to negatively impact the patient's ability to function at work, school, socially, or in other important areas of the patient's life (burlingame, 2001).

- personality disorders: ingrained and inflexible maladaptive patterns of thinking and acting that limit a person's ability to function in society by limiting their potential. Some more common personality disorders are borderline, antisocial, and passive-aggressive.

• schizophrenia: an organically based set of mental disorders in which the patient demonstrates at least two of the following: delusions, hallucinations, disorganized speech, disorganized or catatonic behaviors, and/or negative symptoms such as a flattening of affect, a lack of speech, or inability or lack of desire to make choices. If the patient is experiencing bizarre active auditory hallucinations or bizarre delusions, the patient is not required to have at least two of the listed symptoms. The symptoms must also be significantly and negatively impacting the patient's ability to function socially and/or vocationally, have lasted at least six months (with symptoms possibly controlled during that time) and not related to a schizoaffective or mood disorder, as a result of substance use or general medical conditions, and not related to pervasive developmental disorder. Schizophrenia has four subtypes: paranoid type (delusions or frequent auditory hallucinations), disorganized type (disorganized speech, behavior, and/or affect), catatonic, or undifferentiated (not fitting into the other three categories) (burlingame, 2001).

Cognitive/Developmental Disabilities

- Alzheimer's disease: organic mental disorder that leads to a general loss of cognitive ability. The loss can be observed as a loss in long-term memory, judgment, abstract thinking, and changes in personality. To meet diagnostic criteria for Alzheimer's type dementia the patient must have developed multiple cognitive deficits that reduce independent functioning. The cognitive loss must be significant and impair the patient's ability to learn new information or to recall information learned previously (burlingame, 2001).

- autism: developmental disorder characterized by abnormal or impaired development in social interaction and communication and limited areas of interest. While many developmental disorders produce autistic-like symptoms, to be accurately diagnosed as having autism, the patient must have qualitative impairments in social interactions; qualitative impairments in communication; and restricted repetitive and stereotyped patterns of behavior, interests, and activities (burlingame, 2001).

- delirium: state of cognitive dysfunction where the patient appears confused, has a decreased ability to attend to stimuli in the environment, and may experience a disconnection with reality (from a mild inability to correctly interpret events to full hallucinations). Delirium may mimic other types of organically caused brain disorders; however, delirium and dementia are not the same things (burlingame, 2001).

- dementia: illness or condition that is marked by a progressive loss of intellectual functions. The individual will demonstrate an up and down course of cognitive ability on a day-to-day and even hour-to-hour basis with an overall decrease in ability month by month (burlingame, 2001).

- mental retardation (MR): substantial limitations in present functioning characterized by significantly below average intellectual functioning, existing concurrently with related limitations in two or more of the following applicable adaptive skill (adaptive functioning) areas: communication, self-care, home living, social skills, community use, self-direction, health and safety, functional academics, leisure, and work. Mental retardation manifests before age 18.

- organic brain syndrome: general category of disorders of cognitive functioning including dementia, delirium, amnesiac syndrome, organic anxiety syndrome, intoxication, and withdrawal. While this term was commonly used prior to 1994, its use should decline. Originally called organic mental syndrome in the *DSM-III-R*, it is not found in the *DSM-IV*. The types of organically caused brain syndromes once grouped under organic mental syndrome are now re-grouped into different categories (burlingame, 2001).

Learning Disabilities

Learning Disabilities (LD) are classified as a variety of minimum brain dysfunction disorders that interfere with the normal learning process in children with normal to above normal IQs. There are three primary categories of learning disabilities: dyslexia (difficulties with reading), dysgraphia (difficulties with writing), and dyscalculia (difficulties with mathematics). The *DSM-IV* divides learning disabilities (*DSM-IV*'s term is "learning disorders") into four categories: reading disorder, mathematics disorder, disorder of written expression, and learning disorder not otherwise specified. No matter how the different types of learning disabilities are divided, the key elements are substantially lower scores on academic and IQ tests and/or a significant limitation related to written expression. Children, youth, and adults with learning disabilities tend to have a harder time adapting to life in the community. Reading basic informational material (time schedules, current events in the paper, instructions on equipment and games, etc.) may be difficult to nearly impossible. Budgeting, balancing a checkbook, and figuring out how much tip to leave at a restaurant may all be impacted by a learning disability. Often a patient will mask his/her disability by indicting that s/he is not interested in the activity when, in reality, s/he is not able to complete the task due to his/her disability. Learning disabilities generally do not disappear as the individual reaches and goes through adulthood. Many employers and instructors find that they need to adapt their methods of giving information so that an adult with a learning disability can assimilate the material (burlingame, 2001).

- Asperger syndrome: a milder variant of autistic disorder. In Asperger's syndrome, children isolate themselves from other people and show eccentric behavior. Impairments show up in two-sided social interactions and non-verbal communications. Clumsiness is seen in both their speech and gross motor behavior. They often are strongly interested in a particular topic to the exclusion of interest in the general culture. Some examples include cars, trains, doorknobs, hinges, cappuccino, meteorology, astronomy, and history.

- attention deficit/hyperactivity disorder (ADHD): Nearly four million school-age children have learning disabilities. Of these, at least 20 percent have a type of disorder that leaves them unable to focus their attention. Some children and adults who have attention disorders appear to daydream excessively. And once you get their attention, they're often easily distracted.

  Children with attention disorders are usually hard to miss. Because of their constant motion and explosive energy, hyperactive children often get into trouble with parents, teachers, and peers.

  By adolescence, physical hyperactivity usually subsides into fidgeting and restlessness. But the problems with attention and concentration often continue into adulthood. At work, adults with ADHD often have trouble organizing tasks or completing their work. They do not seem to listen to or follow directions. Their work may be messy and appear careless.

  ADHD has three types: primarily attention deficit (attention deficit hyperactivity disorder, predominately inattention type), primarily hyperactivity (attention deficit hyperactivity disorder, predominately hyperactivity type), or both attention deficit and hyperactivity (attention deficit hyperactivity disorder, combined type). In all three cases the behaviors must be age-inappropriate, evident for at least six months and must be severe enough to negatively impact function at school, home, and/or work. Some of the behaviors must have been present before the person was seven years old (burlingame, 2001).

• other learning disabilities: additional categories, such as "motor skills disorders" and "specific developmental disorders not otherwise specified." These diagnoses include delays in acquiring language, academic, and motor skills that can affect the ability to learn, but do not meet the criteria for a specific learning disability. Also included are coordination disorders that can lead to poor penmanship, as well as certain spelling and memory disorders.

Hearing Disorders

- central deafness: hearing loss caused by a problem in the brainstem or cerebral cortex. People with this disorder will have trouble processing and/or interpreting auditory stimuli. Children with this disorder will often have trouble reading.

- conductive hearing impairment: hearing loss is caused by interference or inadequate conduction of sound through the external or middle ear to the inner ear. Sensitivity to sound is diminished although clarity remains unchanged.

- congenital hearing loss: loss of hearing existing at the time of birth, although it could be developed beforehand. May be hereditary or developed as a result of events during pregnancy.

- deafness: the general term for a condition that is a result of severe or profound hearing loss without naming the degree or cause of the loss.

- hearing impairment: decreased ability to hear sounds. The sensation of hearing is made up of two components: 1. the ability to perceive a range of volumes (loud to soft) and 2. the ability to perceive a range of pitches (do-ra-me-fa-so-la-te-do). When a professional sees an individual with a hearing loss, the loss will be described by the part of the ear that is damaged: 1. conductive (damage to the outer or middle ear), 2. sensorineural (damage to the inner ear or to the auditory nerve), or 3. mixed (a combination of both conductive and sensorineural). A sensorineural hearing loss is seldom correctable by medication and/or surgery, requiring instead the use of a hearing aid and/or sign language. A loss of the ability to hear sounds in one's environment is a significant loss. The primary concerns to be addressed by the professional are 1. social isolation, 2. communication impairment, and 3. loss of normal (hearing) development, even with early intervention (burlingame, 2001).

- sensorineural hearing impairment: condition in which sounds move correctly through the external and middle ear, but defects in either the inner ear or auditory nerve result in hearing loss. Sounds may be unclear, a problem that is sometimes remedied by their amplification.

Visual Disabilities

- amblyopia: loss of visual function not caused by refractive errors or by an organic disease. In layman's terms, this disorder is frequently called "lazy eye" and is typically the result of a congenital defect or a traumatic accident. Other possible causes are poisons like lead or quinine (burlingame, 2001).

- blindness: lack of visual perception due to physiological or psychological factors. It may be used to refer to a complete loss or a partial loss of vision.

- cataract: common cause of reduced vision, especially in individuals over the age of 70, formed as the lens of the eye becomes harder and more opaque. In cases of cataracts where trauma or congenital pathology is not the cause, the disease usually progresses in each eye, although not at the same rate. Surgery is successful in about 98% of the individuals who undergo surgery to remove the natural lens and replace it with a plastic one (burlingame, 2001).

- diplopia: double vision. The person that has this disability will see a double perception of any image (horizontally, vertically, or diagonally). The brain tries to suppress one of these images as a survival mechanism, but vision in one eye may be lost as a result of this suppression.

- glaucoma: disease of the eye that produces increased intraocular pressure. Prolonged periods of increased pressure without treatment may lead to visual impairment and eventually blindness (burlingame, 2001).

- legal blindness: having, in the better eye, vision worse than 20/200 (or 6/60) with corrective lenses and a viewing angle of no greater than 20 degrees.

- night blindness: inability to see well in the darkness of night or under conditions of reduced illumination due to many factors including deficiency of rhodopsin in the rods of the eye.

- tunnel vision: loss of peripheral vision with retention of the central vision that can be caused by many things including advanced chronic glaucoma. The effect is that of looking through a hollow tube (or tunnel).

- visual impairment: The ability to see is a seven-step process. If there is an interruption or malfunction in any of the seven steps, the individual will experience a visual impairment. The degree of impairment, even after treatment, depends on which step is impaired and to what degree. Since information that we receive visually is one of our greatest learning and survival tools, any loss of function changes the way we interact with the world around us (burlingame, 2001).

Chapter Six

Conclusion

Donald R. Snyder
Cyndy Chamberland

Concluding Remarks and Implications for the Future

This text is meant to serve as a starting point and reference for outdoor recreation staff, therapeutic recreation specialists, rehabilitation counselors, students, and others in both the public and private sector interested in adapting outdoor recreation programs to serve individuals with varied disabilities. While this text includes a variety of outdoor recreation activities that can be adapted to include persons with disabilities, it by no means covers the entire spectrum of outdoor recreation activities that can also be adapted. White water rafting, water skiing, fly fishing, hunting, archery, sledding, swimming, rock climbing,

ATV trail riding, horseback riding, sailing, scuba diving, jet skiing, bird watching, down-hill skiing, mountain biking, orienteering, wilderness camping, and more can also be adapted to be inclusive so persons with disabilities can participate.

Because persons with disabilities have unique situations in terms of their disabilities, there cannot be a cookie cutter approach to designing accessible inclusive outdoor recreation programs. Above all, it is most important to learn the capabilities and needs of each participant. It is helpful if staff are familiar with a wide range of disability conditions including those that are physical, cognitive, visual, auditory, and psychiatric in nature. Staff should also be aware of disability etiquette and strive to treat each person who has a disability with respect. Adaptations will sometimes work beautifully and other times not well at all, again depending on the individual's capabilities and needs. Patience, creativity, flexibility, motivation, and genuine interest from the staff in including persons with disabilities in programs are fundamental.

When first starting out to design and deliver accessible outdoor recreation programs, Shared Ventures Outdoors staff learned that it is best to start small. We recommend that one particular activity be introduced at a time with a small group of persons with and without disabilities. This will enable staff and volunteers to focus on one activity with participants and develop experience and competencies in adapting the activity for individuals with disabilities. For example, if an organization already provides ice-skating and wants to begin including persons with disabilities in the program, the organization might start with integrating accessible ice-skating into their program. The organization could purchase a few accessible ice sleds, ice walkers, and shortened hockey sticks with picks and introduce this adapted equipment into the program.

Getting the word out to the disabled community is also a critical component when developing adaptive recreation programs. Publicity needs to happen through various methods in order to reach persons with disabilities, family members, and organizations that serve persons with disabilities. When starting up a new adaptive outdoor recreation program, organizations can develop press releases and send them to newspapers, radio, and television stations. Organizations can follow up with the media by calling editors of newspapers and television news to encourage them to do a story about the program featuring the adaptive component. Flyers and newsletters can also be developed and sent to organizations and agencies that serve persons with disabilities and families. Flyers can be posted in prominent places in the community such as libraries, shopping centers, community centers, etc. The internet is another excellent source for publicity. And, of course, word of mouth is the best method. Organizations can advertise their program on their web site as well as on other web sites. Staff can also do presentations about the program to organizations that serve persons with disabilities. It can take some time to get a program off the ground. With dedication, effort, and ongoing publicity, persons with disabilities will begin to take notice, make inquiries, and start attending.

Evaluation is also an important component when developing adaptive recreation programs. Staff and participants should be encouraged to provide ongoing feedback about the strengths and weaknesses of the program, both informally and formally. Staff and volunteers should make the effort to check in with new participants at the end of programs and hear what the experience was like for them. Did they enjoy the activity? If adaptations were needed, did they work adequately? What are the participants' recommendations for improving the program? Participants who have attended more regularly can complete anonymous evaluation forms and mail them back to the staff in the organization's self-addressed, stamped envelope.

Outdoor recreation can provide individuals with opportunities to challenge themselves, socialize, develop new skills and interests, get exercise, enhance their well being, and enjoy leisure. These same benefits apply to persons with disabilities who participate in outdoor recreation activities. Participants with disabilities typically also experience greater independence, feelings of equality, and a personal sense of empowerment when mastering outdoor recreation activities. It is exciting that outdoor recreation of all types is becoming more accessible to persons with all kinds of disabilities.

Remember to work with abilities and build bridges to overcome the biopsychosocial barriers that have prevented thousands of persons with disabilities from enjoying the great outdoors. Modifications and adaptations using Snyder's Five-Point Diagram is a simple, but thorough means to ensure that a quality experience is provided with a risk management plan to meet the needs and interest of the individual and group. Hopefully this manual will inspire hundreds of organizations, agencies, parks, and businesses to adapt outdoor recreation programs and make their programs accessible for all.

Appendices

A. How the Universal Access Program works in a State Park System

B. Massachusetts State Parks Survey for People with Disabilities

C. Massachusetts Department of Environmental Management Survey for People with Disabilities-January 2001

D. Other Resources: Equipment Resources List, Website Resources List

A: How the Universal Access Program Works in a State Park System

The Department of Conservation and Recreation is organized into five regions within the Commonwealth of Massachusetts, with a primary administrative office in the Boston area.

Each region has a regional headquarters and staff to oversee the administration and management of parks, forest lands, and facilities within the region. Engineers, foresters, fire patrol, rangers, program coordinators, and administrative staff, as well as a regional director, are associated with every region.

Each park has a supervisor and one to five year-round employees and one to ten seasonal employees to fulfill the staffing and management requirements at each park. Park staff responsibilities may include campground management, grounds keeping, building maintenance, receiving the public at the front gate, beach maintenance, life guarding, and interpretation of natural and historic resources. Regional meetings are held once a month to keep park staff informed and cohesive regarding operational procedures, policies, and upcoming changes.

The Universal Access Program is a small program within DCR, organized as part of the Human Resources division of DCR's Boston office. It operates out of one region as a satellite, with statewide responsibilities for employee accommodations, site improvements, equipment distribution, staff awareness and training, and program implementation. Staff varies from three to six people, depending on funding. In addition, the program utilizes one to three seasonal employees, one to two interns, and contracted staff as feasible.

Universal Access Program — Management of Accessible Recreation Programs

Defining staff roles and responsibilities has enabled the DCR to coordinate and expand accessible recreation programs throughout Massachusetts. The following positions have been developed to ensure DCR's mission of making the parks accessible to all citizens.

- *Program Director*: budget management, program direction, staff management
- *Program Coordinator*: coordinate yearly program schedule, purchase and maintain equipment, coordinate program staff, communication liaison with park staff, coordinate publicity and outreach, oversee program development
- *Grant Coordinator*: research and write grants, data collection and reports for grant documentation, research and development of new funding sources, assist with program development
- *Recreation Facilitator* (under Shared Ventures Outdoors grant): assist in recreation programs as needed, oversee grad associate or intern, outreach tasks, office tasks
- *Grad Associate or Intern* (under Shared Ventures Outdoors grant): assist in recreation programs as needed, office tasks, special projects related to educational goals

Universal Access Program Equipment

Adaptive recreation equipment is purchased through the state procurement system, according to specifications researched and ideally tested in advance by Universal Access Program staff. Equipment is maintained and distributed by Universal Access Program staff. In many instances, equipment is housed seasonally or year round at various park facilities.

Recreation Program Leadership and Staff

Recreation organizations or outdoor leaders are hired to facilitate recreation programs through a contract arrangement. Universal Access Program staff may assist at programs as needed. Volunteers are utilized in recreation programs to assist with activities.

General Risk Management

The following guidelines are used for successful risk management:
- Participants sign waivers as an acknowledgement of risk and to protect the state against unfair or unrealistic lawsuits.
- Participants follow safety rules and regulations established in the programs, such as wearing a lifejacket while boating and proper clothing for winter activities.
- Program staff must be qualified outdoor leaders, with a minimum of First Aid and CPR training, with professional experience or appropriate certification in the instruction of recreation activities they will facilitate.
- Program staff must have liability insurance, provided by the recreation organization or company for which they work.

- Program staff are trained to monitor participant behavior, equipment conditions, weather, etc. and act to minimize risk when necessary.
- Program staff are trained to have communication access (radios are provided) to park staff on duty while program is taking place. In the event of accident or injury, the park's emergency management plan would be activated.
- DCR Rangers are usually present at larger programs and events to assist with parking, traffic, crowd management, and emergency issues.

General Program Evaluation Methods (for any activity)

The following methods are used to provide documentation and analysis of programs:

- Program leaders complete one-page session reports after every program so consistent data can be collected.
- Program leaders write a seasonal report providing documentation on an entire recreation season with recommendations for future improvements.
- Program coordinator assesses data and information from reports and staff communications and makes adjustments with regard to equipment, staffing, scheduling, outreach methods, safety, accessibility needs, etc.
- Program coordinator creates seasonal or yearly recreation reports compiling data and information for long-term planning and budgeting purposes.
- Shared Ventures Outdoors staff conducts participant surveys to determine responses to recreation programs such as

improvements in self-esteem, independence, skill level, etc.

- Shared Ventures Outdoors staff analyzes survey results to create final reports on benefits of recreation for people with disabilities.
- An accessibility evaluation is available to the public to register comments on parks and programs.

Outreach Strategies

Outreach strategies are generally consistent for any given recreation activity or season:

- Programs are posted on DCR's website: http://www.mass.gov/dcr/
- Press releases are sent to newspaper calendars and features editors, TV, and radio stations.
- DCR publishes a twice-yearly newsletter, Access News, which features program achievements and upcoming calendars.
- Direct mailings of newsletters and seasonal flyers take place two to three times per year.
- Program flyers are posted in the parks where programs will occur.
- Presentations are made to disability groups and organizations.
- Phone calls are made to interested individuals, families, and groups to invite them to attend upcoming programs. (This is critical to ensure attendance.)

B: Survey

Massachusetts State Parks Survey
For People with Disabilities

1. Name: (optional) _____

2. Address: (optional) _____

Town: _____ Zip Code: _____

Phone: (optional) _____ E-mail: _____

3. Gender of survey respondent.
       ____ Male   ____ Female

4. Which category best describes the age group of the individual with a disability.

___ 0-5	___ 17-22	___ 36-40	___ 51-55	___ 66+
___ 6-11	___ 23-30	___ 41-45	___ 56-60	
___ 12-16	___ 31-35	___ 46-50	___ 61-65	

5. What is your marital status?

___ Single ___ Married ___ Partnered ___ Divorced ___ Widowed

6. Do you have any children? ___ Yes ___ No
       Ages 2-5 6-12 13-18 18+

7. Which category best describes your annual household income?
       ___ under $15,000   ___ $ 59,000 - $ 69,999
       ___ $ 15,000 - $ 25,999   ___ $ 70,000 - $ 80,999
       ___ $ 26,000 - $ 36,999   ___ $ 81,000 - $100,000
       ___ $ 37,000 - $ 47,999   ___ $100,000 +
       ___ $ 48,000 - $ 58,999

8. Which category best describes your present living situation?
   ___ Live independently
   ___ Live independently with a personal care attendant
   ___ Live independently with a roommate/s
   ___ Live with spouse/partner
   ___ Live in a group residence
   ___ Live with parents or family member(s)
   ___ Other (please specify) _____

9. Which category best describes the person who makes the decision to recreate. Please check all that apply.

___ Self ___ Father ___ Mother ___ Sibling ___ Guardian
___ Human service worker ___ Spouse/Partner
___ Other (please specify) _____

10. Which best describes the respondent's condition/disability. Please check all that apply.

___ Legally Blind	___ Amputee	___ Muscular Dystrophy
___ Visually Impaired	___ Arthritis	___ Spina Bifida
___ Deaf	___ Cerebral Palsy	___ Spinal Cord Injury
___ Hearing Impaired	___ Chemical Dependency	___ Stroke
___ Mental Retardation	___ Chemical Sensitivity	___ Chronic Fatigue
___ Learning Disability	___ Traumatic Brain Injury	___ Heart Condition
___ Behavioral	___ Emotional/Psychological	
___ Other: (please specify) _____		

11. Which of the following activities are you interested in? Please check all that apply.

___ Rock climbing	___ Hiking	___ Nature walks
___ Camping	___ Backpacking	___ Jogging
___ Ice-skating	___ Swimming	___ Running
___ Wilderness camping	___ Fishing	___ Orienteering
___ Snow shoeing	___ Horseback riding	___ Festivals & events
___ Cycling	___ Bird watching	___ Hunting
___ Mountain biking	___ Photography	___ Outdoor concerts
___ Cross-country sit-skiing	___ Boating	___ Playground activity
___ Downhill skiing	___ Walking	___ Walking
___ Canoeing	___ Kayaking	___ Picnicking

Camping	Swimming	Sports activity: (please specify)
___ Tent	___ Pools	_____
___ Recreational vehicle	___ Fresh water	_____
___ Wilderness	___ Ocean	_____
___ Cabin	Other (please specify)	_____

12. Please answer the following question. Check all that apply.

      I don't participate in recreational activities because:
      ___ Don't have time
      ___ Don't have transportation
      ___ Family obligations
      ___ Fatigue
      ___ Lack of support
      ___ Lack of experience
      ___ My disability/condition
      ___ I am not interested
Other (please specify) _____

13. Have you recreated in a Massachusetts State Park?

      ___ Yes (Please proceed to questions 14 - 22)
      ___ No (Please proceed to questions 17 - 22)

      If yes, what is the year of your most recent use? _____

14. Which of the following recreation activities have you participated in a Massachusetts State Park? Check all that apply.

      Independent use of Massachusetts State Parks:

___ Picnicking	___ Fishing
___ Trails	___ Boating
___ Camping	___ Swimming
___ ATV/snowmobile	___ Other (please specify) _____

      Education/Interpretive program:

___ Nature walks	___ Historical tours
___ Crafts	___ Other (please specify) _____
___ Presentations	

Universal Access programs:

___ Adaptive rowing   ___ Adaptive canoeing/kayaking
___ Cross-country skiing   ___ Ice-skating with ice sleds
___ Seasonal accessible recreation events
___ Other (please specify) _____

Independent use of adaptive recreational equipment in Massachusetts
State Parks:

___ Pool lifts   ___ Ice sleds
___ Beach wheelchairs   ___ Handcycles
___ Cross-country sit-skis
___ Other (please specify) _____

Cultural programs:

___ Concerts/performances ___ Festivals
___ Seasonal events
___ Other (please specify) _____

Competitive events:
Please describe _____

Group activities:
Please describe _____

15. Which Massachusetts State Park have you visited and enjoyed? Please name
each site.

1._____   4._____
2._____   5._____
3._____   6._____

16. From your previous experience in a Massachusetts State Park setting, which
of the following barriers have you encountered? Please check all that apply.

___ Rough pathways   ___ Narrow paths
___ Curbs or steps   ___ Steep grades
___ Points of interest not accessible   ___ Park activities not accessible
___ Recreation areas not accessible   ___ Lack of accessible restrooms
___ Lack of signage   ___ Lack of adaptive equipment
___ No signage in Braille   ___ No information in large print

___ Not enough points of interest   ___ No benches/resting places
___ No information in Braille   ___ No sign language interpretation
___ No assistance provided   ___ Staff sensitivity
Other (please specify) _____

If you do not utilize Massachusetts State Parks and their programs (answered
"no" to question 14), please continue here.

17. Which of the following factors are problematic to you with regard to a
Massachusetts State Park?
___ Cost   ___ Knowledgeable staff
___ Lack of specialized equipment ___ Transportation
___ Distance   `   ___ Lack of awareness of program offerings
___ Lack of time   ___ Lack of accessibility
___ Inadequate services/amenities   ___ No opportunity
___ Uninterested   ___ Lack of someone to recreate with
___ Lack of assistance   ___ Safety

18. Please indicate what areas that the Massachusetts State Parks could improve
upon which would prompt you to reconsider utilizing their programs. Please
check all that apply.

___ Increasing accessible trails   ___ Directions to parks
___ More reasonable cost   ___ Signage to parks
___ Publicity of accessible activities and locations   ___ More bike paths
___ Cleanliness of park facility   ___ More programs
___ Improved accessibility at facilities   ___ More staff
___ More adaptive recreation equipment   ___ More scenic views
___ Availability of maps, brochures
___ Increase staff awareness
___ Other (please specify) _____

19. Please indicate the best method to reach you. Please check all that apply.

___ Television   ___ Phone call update
___ Radio   ___ E-mail notification
___ Local newspaper   ___ Direct mailing
___ Web site   ___ Support group meeting
___ Flyers posted in parks   ___ Newsletter
___ Other (please specify) _____

20. Which of the following activities are you interested in if provided as an accessible program in a Massachusetts State Park?

___ Ice-skating   ___ Paddleboating   ___ Nature education
___ Camping   ___ Cross county skiing   ___ Snowmobiling
___ Fishing   ___ Rowing   ___ All-terrain vehicles
___ Hiking   ___ Bicycling   ___ Ropes course
___ Swimming   ___ Rock climbing   ___ Photography
___ Horseback riding   ___ Sailing   ___ Waterskiing
___ Orienteering   ___ Canoeing/kayaking
___ Other (please specify) _____

21. Would you like to be included on our mailing list and notified about accessible recreation opportunities?

           ___ Yes   ___ No

22. Would you like to offer more specific feedback about your needs and interests in accessible recreation programs at a later date in a Department of Conservation and Recreation meeting?

           ___ Yes   ___ No

Thank you for your time in answering these questions!

C: Massachusetts DCR Survey for People with Disabilities

In 2002 an outdoor recreation survey was given to persons with disabilities throughout the state of Massachusetts, as shown in Appendix B. One hundred fifty-six persons completed the survey. Based on respondent's answers, various factors were identified that impact individuals with disabilities' participation in outdoor recreation, especially at MA State Parks. The following report contains conclusions from the survey.

Factors identified by survey respondents explaining why they don't participate in outdoor recreation activities (N=156)

1. Disability/condition	73	46.79%
2. Transportation	43	27.56%
3. Fatigue	26	16.67%
4. Lack of support	26	16.67%
5. Lack of experience	25	16.03%
6. Don't have time	15	9.62%
7. Family obligations	14	8.97%
8. Not interested	4	2.56%

The significant number of non-users who list their disability/condition as a factor to recreating (47%) may not be aware of adaptations in accessible recreation that could enable them to participate. Transportation is also a significant problem. Lack of experience, support, and fatigue are also major factors.

Respondents Use at MA State Parks

Ninety-five of the 156 respondents (60%) reported they had recreated in a Massachusetts State Park. Sixty-one respondents (39%) reported they had not. It should be noted however that for the 95 respondents who reported using MA State Parks, 25 parks that were mentioned are not classified as MA State Parks, but were municipal, private, or other types of parks. All together 69 parks were named and of these, 44 represented DCR MA State Parks. The parks named covered a wide geographic area in the state including the Berkshires, the Boston area, Cape Cod, Franklin County, Hampshire County, Worcester area, and Hampden County. Hampden County was the most popular of the respondents with 20 parks named. This is attributed to the close proximity to the majority of the survey respondents' residence. One Connecticut park was also named. Other significant findings include the following:

- DAR State Forest had the most frequent usage with 21 visits.
- Chicopee State Park was second with 13 visits.
- Dunn Pond State Park and Lake Dennison were third with ten visits each.
- Mohawk Trail, Wendell State Forest, and Forest Park (a non-state park) tied for fourth, each having six visits.

Recreation Activities Participation by MA State Park Users

Independent Use of MA State Parks

The most popular activities named in this category were as follows:

- Picnicking was named by 68 users (43.59%).
- Trails were named by 37 users (23.72%).
- Swimming was named by 31 users (19.87%).
- Boating was named by 26 users (16.67%).
- Camping was named by 23 users (14.74%).
- Fishing was named by 12 users (7.69%).

Education/Interpretive Programs

The most popular activities named in this category were as follows:

- Nature walks were named by 20 users (12.82%).
- Historical tours were named by 13 users (8.33%).
- Crafts and Presentations were each named by six users (3.85%).

Universal Access Programs

- Seasonal Recreation Events and Adaptive Canoeing/Kayaking each were named by 21 users (13.46%).
- Adaptive Rowing was named by 15 users (9.62%).
- Cross-Country Skiing was named by eleven users (7.05%).
- Sled Skating was named by nine users (5.77%).

Independent Use of Adaptive Recreational Equipment

- Handcycles was named by twelve users (7.69%).
- Beach wheelchairs were named by eight users (5.13%).
- Cross-country skis and ice sleds were each named by five users (3.21%).
- Pool lifts were named by two users (1.28%).

Cultural Programs
- Festivals were named by 15 users (9.62%).
- Concerts/performances and Seasonal Events each were named by 14 users (8.97%).

Competitive Events
Comments by users included the following:
- None available
- Canoeing
- Bluefishing
- Basketball

Group Activities
Several users described various group activities they took part in at MA State Parks. Group activities included:
- Visiting park with Shake a Leg Program
- Touring Rock Quarry
- Picnics
- Demos
- Swimming
- Camping
- Church Services
- Strolling/Walking
- Canoeing
- Canoe Trip
- Outdoor Explorations

Massachusetts State Park Visitation by Users

Users reported a total of 178 visits that occurred at 69 parks, 44 of which are MA State Parks. There is some confusion by users as to which parks they visited were MA State Parks as 25 named were not MA State Parks.

Significant findings are as follows:

Berkshire Area

- Users visited twelve different parks, eleven of which are MA State Parks. Total number of visits: 45.
- Most frequented park: DAR with 21 visits.
- Mohawk Trail SF listed six visits.
- Mt. Greylock SP listed four visits.
- Beartown SF, Florida, Hawley, North Adams SP, Pittsfield SF, Savoy, Tolland SF, and Windsor each listed one or two visits.
- Chesterfield Gorge a non-MA State Park was listed with one visit.

Boston Area

- Users visited six different parks, all of which are MA State Parks.
- Total number of visits: nine.
- The six parks listed each received one or two visits.
- Cochituate SP, Harold Parkert SF, and Walden Pond SP each listed two visits.

- Borderland SP, Callahan SP, and Hopkington SP each listed one visit.

Cape Cod Area

- Users visited five different parks, four of which are MA State Parks and one that is questionable.
- Cape Cod National Seashore received two visits.
- Horseneck Beach, Myles Standish Monument, and Watson Pond each received one visit.
- Brewster received one visit.

Franklin County Area

- Users visited seven different parks, six of which are MA State Parks.
- Total number of visits: 27.
- Most frequented park was Dunn Pond SP, with ten visits. It should be noted however that surveys were available at Dunn Pond SP during the ADA Celebration and this probably accounts for the higher number of visits at Dunn Pond SP.
- Wendell SF received six visits.
- Lake Wyola and Erving SF each received four visits.
- Gardner Heritage SP, Mt. Toby each received one visit.
- Barton's Cove a non-MA State Park received one visit.

Hampden County Area

- Users visited 20 different parks, eight of which are MA State Parks.
- Total number of visits: 59 (36 visits in the eight MA State Parks).

- Most frequented park was Chicopee SP with 13 visits.
- Robinson SP received seven visits.
- Forest Park, a municipal park in Springfield received six visits.
- Skinner SP and Stanley Park (a non-MA State Park each received four visits.
- Mt. Holyoke Range and Mt. Tom State Reservation each received three visits.
- Dean Pond, Hampden Ponds SP, and Holyoke Heritage SP each received two visits.
- Blunt Park, Five Mile Pond, Holland Pond, Ludlow, Massasoit, Mitteneague, Six Flags Szot Park, Van Horn Park, and Westfield each received one to two visits and are all non-MA State Parks.

Hampshire County Area

- Users visited twelve different parks, three of which are MA State Parks and nine of which are non-MA State Parks or questionable.
- Total number of visits: 25 (13 visits occurred in a MA State Park).
- Most frequented park listed was Norwottuck Rail Trail with seven visits.
- Connecticut River Greenway/Elwell received four visits.
- Look Park, a municipal park in Florence received three visits.
- Mt. Sugarloaf and Quabbin Reservoir (a non-MA State Park) each received two visits.
- Catamount, Dubuque, Historical Valley Campground, Howe, MDA, Mills River and Orastes all of which are non-MA State Parks or questionable each received one visit.

Worcester Area

- Users visited six different parks all of which are MA State Parks.
- Total number of visits: six.
- Lake Dennison, Pearl Hill, Purgatory Chasm, Mt. Wachusetts, Rutland SP, and Wells SP each received one visit.

Barriers Encountered at MA State Parks as Defined by Users

Barriers to recreating at MA State Parks listed by the 95 users are as follows starting with the most severe: (N=95)

Barrier	# of Users	% of Users
1. Rough paths	42	44%
2. Steep grades	32	34%
3. Lack of accessible restrooms	30	32%
4. Points not accessible	27	28%
5. Curbs/steps	25	26%
6. No assistance provided	19	20%
7. Lack of adaptive equipment	18	19%
8. Activities not accessible	16	17%
9. No benches/resting places	15	16%
10. Not enough points of interest	14	15%
11. Recreation not accessible	12	13%
12. Staff sensitivity	11	12%
13. Lack of signage	10	11%
14. No information in large print	5	5%
15. No information in Braille	3	3%
16. No sign language interpreter	3	3%

17. No signage in Braille   2   2%

Other barriers mentioned by users include:
- Lack of sighted guides
- Lack of transportation
- Lack of Spanish speaking assistance and information in Spanish
- Heavy woodstove/charcoal fumes and pesticides at DAR
- Diesel fumes at Mohawk Trail
- Physical pain
- Inaccessible beaches
- Lack of accessible restrooms and have to travel uphill to access restrooms

One user commented that the MA State Parks are usually excellent.

Problematic Factors identified by the 61 non-users are listed below starting with the most severe: (N=61)

Problematic Factor	# of Non-Users	% of Non-Users
1. Lack awareness of programs	44	72%
2. Transportation	42	69%
3. Lack recreation partner	41	67%
4. Distance	32	52%
5. Cost	32	52%
6. Lack of assistance	28	46%
7. Lack of accessibility	24	39%
8. Lack of specialized equipment	22	36%
9. Lack of time	15	25%
10. Inadequate services/amenities	10	16%
11. No opportunity	10	16%
12. Safety	9	15%

13. Knowledgeable staff	8	13%
14. Not interested	5	8%

Park improvements identified by non-users that would encourage their use of MA State Parks (N-61)

Improvement	# of Non-Users	% of Non-Users
1. More accessible trails	48	79%
2. Better publicity	41	67%
3. Improved accessibility	34	56%
4. More programs	29	48%
5. More reasonable cost	28	46%
6. More adaptive equipment	26	43%
7. Availability of maps/brochures	20	33%
8. Directions to parks	19	31%
9. More scenic views	17	28%
10. More staff	17	28%
11. Increased staff awareness	17	28%
12. Cleanliness	16	26%
13. More bike paths	12	20%
14. Signage to parks	11	18%

Other recommended park improvements listed by non-users

- Week time events conflict with work
- No RV facilities with complete hookups in western MA
- Need more toilets and showers
- Need more activities in Franklin County
- More restrooms so people don't have to walk so far
- More open restrooms
- No dogs allowed off leash

- Better security
- Scent free areas to hike, camp, swim
- More trails and swim areas away from congested areas
- More rental equipment for PWDs e.g. hand cycles, tandems, boats, fishing
- Knowing which parks are accessible for their disability
- Area for service dog bathroom
- Sensitivity training
- More parks closer to Boston
- Bigger restrooms
- More accessible beaches
- Signage at forks in trails, closest to parking lot
- Transportation
- Someone to recreate with
- Public transportation
- Programs at more locations with expanded hours to use (e.g. not three to five but nine to eight)

Activities most interested in at MA State Parks (N=156)

Activity	# of Respondents	% of Respondents
1. Swimming	67	43%
2. Camping	59	38%
3. Canoe/kayak	53	34%
4. Horseback riding	52	33%
5. Fishing	50	32%
6. Nature education	49	31%
7. Hiking	42	27%
8. Paddleboats	42	27%
9. Sailing	42	27%
10. Bicycling	39	25%

11. ATV's	37	24%
12. Photography	35	22%
13. Rowing	25	16%
14. Cross-country Skiing	24	15%
15. Snowmobiling	23	15%
16. Waterskiing	23	15%
17. Orienteering	20	13%
18. Ice-skating	17	11%
19. Ropes course	16	10%
20. Rock climbing	15	10%

D: Resources

Equipment Resource List

ICE SLEDS
Unique Inventions, Inc.
559 Chamberlain St.
Peterborough, ON
Canada K9J 4L6
705-743-6544
888-886-0881
www.uniqueinventionsinc.com

RECREATION EQUIPMENT
Access to Recreation
8 Sandra Court
Newbury Park, CA 91320
800-634-4351
www.accesstr.com

SIT-SKIS
Spokes 'n Motion
2226 South Jason Street
Denver, CO 80223
303-922-0605
info@spokesnmotion.com
www.spokesnmotion.com

KAYAK HAND ADAPTATION
Bike-On.com
The handcycle store and a whole
lot more!
54 Tiffany Road
Coventry, RI 02816
888-424-5366

**BICYCLES AND BEACH
CHAIRS**
Ultimate Mobility, Inc.
1158 Main Street
Worcester, MA 01603
888-675-1777
www.ultimatemobility.net
info@ultimatemobility.net

HANDCYCLES
Bike-On.com
The handcycle store and a whole
lot more!
54 Tiffany Road
Coventry, RI 02816
888-424-5366

WHEELCHAIR TANDEM BIKE
Frank Mobility
1003 International Drive
Oakdale, PA 15071
724-695-7822
888-426-8581
www.frankmobility.com
info@frankmobility.com

FISHING GEAR
Bass Pro
(Multiple Store Locations)
www.basspro.com

FOAM
Nanthahala Outdoor Center
13077 Hwy 19 West
Bryson City, NC 28713
888-905-7238

Danmar Products, Inc.
221 Jackson Industrial Drive
Ann Arbor, MI 48104
800-783-1998

Website Resources

Used in the course of the Shared Ventures Outdoors grant or highly recommended.

ADA Guidelines and Standards:
Access Board: Federal guidelines for all aspects of built and outdoor environments.
www.access-board.gov/

National Center on Accessibility: training and programs addressing recreation, parks, and tourism.
www.indiana.edu/~nca/

Adaptive Outdoor Recreation:
Massachusetts Department of Conservation and Recreation Universal Access Program: Statewide Accessible Recreation Opportunities
www.mass.gov/dcr/universal_access

All Out Adventures: Inclusive outdoor adventure organization based in western Massachusetts
www.alloutadventures.org

Maine Handicapped Skiing: Downhill and cross-country skiing.
www.skimhs.org

Northeast Passage: Barrier free outdoor recreation programs in New England including cycling, sled hockey, hiking, water skiing, scuba diving, and more.
www.nepassage.org/

Outdoor Explorations: Inclusive outdoor adventure organization based in eastern Massachusetts specializing in school programs, kayaking, overnight trips, environmental work projects.
www.outdoorexplorations.org

Vermont Adapted Ski and Sports: Downhill skiing and more in the Green Mountain State.
www.vermontadaptive.org/

Wilderness Inquiry: Inclusive backcountry trips by canoe, kayak, horseback, and foot in North America and beyond.
www.wildemessinquiry.org/

Assistive Technology:
Abledata: Adaptive product directory and reviews
www.abledata.com./

Disability Services:
Check your local disability advocacy, support, and social organizations, as well as state agencies and national disability organizations with local chapters.

Stavros Independent Living Center. Serving western Massachusetts
www.stavros.org

Higher Education:
Springfield College: Undergrad and grad programs in Therapeutic Recreation, Outdoor Recreation, and Sports Management
www.spfldcol.edu/home.nsf/home

Hampshire College: Applied Design program for Assistive Technology
www.hampshire.edu/cms/index.php?id=2927

Greenfield Community College: Outdoor Leadership Program: One-year certification program
www.olp.gcc.mass.edu

Natural and Cultural History Accessible Interpretive Techniques
Part of Your General Public is Disabled: Smithsonian handbook and video
www.astc.org/resource/access/index

National Center on Accessibility: Interpretive training addressing accessibility for people with disabilities in both indoor and outdoor settings.
www.indiana.edu/~nca/

Professional Organizations:
National Parks and Recreation Association (NRPA)
www.nrpa.org

National Therapeutic Recreation Society (NTRS): A branch of the NRPA specializing in clinical and community-based therapeutic recreation
www.nrpa.org

American Therapeutic Recreation Association (ATRA)
www.atra-tr.org

Association for Experiential Education: Therapeutic Adventure (AEE) Professional Group
www.aee.org

Sports:
Check for organized wheelchair sports clubs in your area

Disabled Sports USA: Nationwide sports rehabilitation programs
www.dsusa.org/

Website Accessibility:
WebABLE
www.webable.com/

Bibliography

Austin, D. R. (2001). *Glossary of recreation therapy and occupational therapy.* State College, PA: Venture Publishing. Inc.

Bullock, C. C., & Mahon, M. J. (1999). *Introduction to recreation services for people with disabilities: A person-centered approach (2nd ed.).* Champaign, IL: Sagamore Publishing.

burlingame, j. (2001). *Idyll Arbor's therapy dictionary.* Ravensdale, WA: Idyll Arbor.

Epperson, M. M. (1977). Families in sudden crisis: Process and intervention in a critical care center. *Social Work, 2:*265-273.

Falvo, D. R., (1999). *Medical and psychosocial aspects of chronic illness and disability.* Gaithersburg, Maryland: Aspen Publishers, Inc.

Howe-Murphy, R., & Charboneau, B. G. (1987). *Therapeutic recreation intervention: An ecological perspective.* Englewood Cliffs, NJ: Prentice-Hall.

Huber, G.P. (1980). *Managerial decision making.* Glenview, IL: Scott, Foresman & Co.

McIntosh, R., and Goeldner, C. (1984). *Tourism: Principles, practices, philosophy.* (4th edition). New York, NY: John Wiley and Sons.

Nash, J. B. (1953). *Philosophy of recreation and leisure.* St. Louis, MO: Mosby.

O'Morrow, G. S., & Carter, M. J. (1997). *Effective management in therapeutic recreation service.* State College, PA: Venture Publishing, Inc.

O'Morrow, G., & Reynolds, R. (1989). *Therapeutic recreation: A helping profession (3rd ed.).* Englewood Cliffs, NJ: Prentice-Hall.

O'Toole, Marie T. (Ed.) (1997). *Miller-Keane encyclopedia dictionary of medicine, nursing, and allied health.* Philadelphia, PA: W.B. Saunders Company.

Spraycar, M. (Ed.). (1995). *PDR medical dictionary.* Montvale, NJ: R. R. Donnelley & Sons Company.

Stumbo, N. J. & Peterson, C. A. *Therapeutic recreation program design: Principles and procedures, fourth edition.* San Francisco: Pearson, Benjamin Cummings.

WebMd. Retrieved April 16, 2002 from http://www.webmd.com.

Index

About the Authors

Donald R. Snyder

Dr. Donald R. Snyder, CTRS, has an EdD in Therapeutic Recreation Management from New York University, an MS in Therapeutic Recreation and a BS Degree in Recreation and Leisure Education from Southern Connecticut State University.

Dr. Snyder has worked as a practitioner, educator, administrator, facility designer, and consultant in Therapeutic Recreation, Sport, Recreation Education, and Leisure Services for 35 years. He has served on the Board of Directors for the National Therapeutic Recreation Society (NTRS), the New England Regional Director for the NTRS, the New England Regional Director for the Society for Park and Recreation Educators, and currently on the State Regional Advisory Council for the NTRS representing the State of Connecticut. He has received numerous national, regional, and state awards in Therapeutic Recreation including his profession's highest national award, the 2000 Distinguished Service Award of the National Therapeutic Recreation Society.

Dr. Snyder served as Chairman of the Department of Recreation & Leisure Services at Springfield College in Springfield, Massachusetts for approximately ten years. For the past thirteen years, Dr. Snyder has served as Professor and Graduate Coordinator for the Department of Sport Management and Recreation at Springfield College. He has served as the clinical internship supervisor for over 23 years and has placed interns in 47 states, Canada, Bermuda, and Puerto Rico. Prior to this, he started Post University's Therapeutic Recreation major in Waterbury, Connecticut and was instrumental in establishing Mitchell College's Associate Degree Program in Therapeutic Recreation in New London, Connecticut. Dr. Snyder also served for seven years as the Coordinator of Therapeutic Recreation and Director of Athletics for the Devereux Foundation in Washington, Connecticut, a nationally known organization serving children with emotional and learning disabilities. He has written numerous grants and has served as a professional reviewer for a number of textbooks used in the field today.

Dr. Snyder has made over 85 international, national, regional, and statewide presentations. He has served as a keynote speaker on Therapeutic Recreation and Facility Design and Management throughout the United States, Puerto Rico, Bermuda, Canada, and Hong Kong (China). Dr. Snyder played a key role in the development of a variety of Springfield College Sport Management and Recreation grants most recently serving as Springfield College's Coordinator for Shared Ventures Outdoors, a Therapeutic Recreation inclusion grant with the Massachusetts Department of Recreation and Conservation from 1999-2002.

During the spring of 2005, he conducted a major facility design study/investigation of recently constructed college/university student and campus recreation centers concentrating on accessibility and access design of premier facilities in New England.

Anne M. Rothschadl

Dr. Anne M. Rothschadl has a PhD from Indiana University in Leisure Behavior and an MA in Park and Recreation Management (Therapeutic Recreation) from the University of Oregon. Dr. Rothschadl has worked as a practitioner in recreation, community education, and outdoor recreation. She is currently an Associate Professor in the Department of Sport Management and Recreation at Springfield College in Springfield, Massachusetts, teaching undergraduate and graduate courses and serves as the research coordinator for the department.

Dr. Rothschadl has served for several years on the Board of Directors of the Leisure and Aging Section (LAS) of the National Recreation and Park Association (NRPA), is the national newsletter editor, and chairs the LAS poster sessions at the yearly NRPA Congress. Dr. Rothschadl has authored a variety of publications and research projects, including co-chairing the NRPA Research Roundtable that set NRPA's national research agenda. She has made numerous scholarly and professional presentations for the National Recreation and Park Association, Canadian Therapeutic Recreation Association annual conference, New England Training Institute, state association conferences, councils on aging, regional and local conferences, and meetings.

Dr. Rothschadl has been an active member and participant in the Shared Ventures Outdoors Inclusion Grant with the Massachusetts Department of Conservation and Recreation.

Marcy Marchello

Marcy Marchello is the Universal Access Program Coordinator for the Massachusetts Department of Conservation and Recreation. She has a distinguished career in providing outdoor recreation and education programs for and with persons with disabilities in the State of Massachusetts. She played a major role in the development, implementation, coordination, and evaluation of the nationally known Massachusetts Shared Ventures Outdoors Recreation Grant, which provides inclusion for persons with disabilities in Massachusetts state parks and forests.

Ms. Marchello has made numerous national, regional, and state presentations on new recreation experiences, successful inclusive outdoor recreation programs, and activities. Her outdoor recreation protocols have helped provide outdoor recreation for hundreds of individuals with disabilities. She was a presenter at the September 2006 National Institute on Recreation Inclusion.

Printed in the United States
57261LVS00002B/16-84